03841

Enhancing Student Development with Computers

Cynthia S. Johnson, K. Richard Pyle, *Editors*

NEW DIRECTIONS FOR STUDENT SERVICES

URSULA DELWORTH and GARY R. HANSON, *Editors-in-Chief*

Number 26, June 1984

Paperback sourcebooks in
The Jossey-Bass Higher Education Series

Jossey-Bass Inc., Publishers
San Francisco • Washington • London

Cynthia S. Johnson, K. Richard Pyle (Eds.).
Enhancing Student Development with Computers.
New Directions for Student Services, no. 26.
San Francisco: Jossey-Bass, 1984.

New Directions for Student Services Series
Ursula Delworth and Gary R. Hanson, *Editors-in-Chief*

New Directions for Student Services (publication number USPS
449-070) is published quarterly by Jossey-Bass Inc., Publishers.
Second-class postage rates paid at San Francisco, California,
and at additional mailing offices.

Correspondence:
Subscriptions, single-issue orders, change of address notices, undelivered
copies, and other correspondence should be sent to Subscriptions,
Jossey-Bass Inc., Publishers, 433 California Street, San Francisco
California 94104.

Editorial correspondence should be sent to the Editors-in-Chief,
Ursula Delworth, University Counseling Service, Iowa
Memorial Union, University of Iowa, Iowa City, Iowa 52242
or Gary R. Hanson, Office of the Dean of Students,
Student Services Building, Room 101, University of Texas
at Austin, Austin, Texas 78712.

Library of Congress Catalogue Card Number LC 83-82740

International Standard Serial Number ISSN 0164-7970

International Standard Book Number ISBN 87589-787-8

Cover art by Willi Baum

Manufactured in the United States of America

Ordering Information

The paperback sourcebooks listed below are published quarterly and can be ordered either by subscription or single-copy.

Subscriptions cost $35.00 per year for institutions, agencies, and libraries. Individuals can subscribe at the special rate of $25.00 per year *if payment is by personal check.* (Note that the full rate of $35.00 applies if payment is by institutional check, even if the subscription is designated for an individual.) Standing orders are accepted. Subscriptions normally begin with the first of the four sourcebooks in the current publication year of the series. When ordering, please indicate if you prefer your subscription to begin with the first issue of the *coming* year.

Single copies are available at $8.95 when payment accompanies order, and *all single-copy orders under $25.00 must include payment.* (California, New Jersey, New York, and Washington, D.C., residents please include appropriate sales tax.) For billed orders, cost per copy is $8.95 plus postage and handling. (Prices subject to change without notice.)

Bulk orders (ten or more copies) of any individual sourcebook are available at the following discounted prices: 10–49 copies, $8.05 each; 50–100 copies, $7.15 each; over 100 copies, *inquire.* Sales tax and postage and handling charges apply as for single copy orders.

To ensure correct and prompt delivery, all orders must give either the *name of an individual* or an *official purchase order number.* Please submit your order as follows:

Subscriptions: specify series and year subscription is to begin.
Single Copies: specify sourcebook code (such as, SS8) and first two words of title.

Mail orders for United States and Possessions, Latin America, Canada, Japan, Australia, and New Zealand to:
Jossey-Bass Inc., Publishers
433 California Street
San Francisco, California 94104

Mail orders for all other parts of the world to:
Jossey-Bass Limited
28 Banner Street
London EC1Y 8QE

New Directions for Student Services Series
Ursula Delworth and Gary R. Hanson, *Editors-in-Chief*

SS1 *Evaluating Program Effectiveness,* Gary R. Hanson
SS2 *Training Competent Staff,* Ursula Delworth
SS3 *Reducing the Dropout Rate,* Lee Noel
SS4 *Applying New Developmental Findings,* Lee Knefelkamp, Carole Widick, Clyde A. Parker

Contents

Editors' Notes

Student affairs professionals have a new tool to assist them in student development — the computer. This tool not only frees educators from repetitive tasks, stores and retrieves vast quantities of information, and provides badly needed assessment capabilities, but it can also teach students decision-making skills and provides other sophisticated assistance in an individualized manner. However, because the profession of student affairs has not been at the forefront of the computer revolution in higher education (applications that relate to administrative functions or instruction have taken precedence), it is only with the advent of the low-cost microcomputer and the recent availability of software packages for student affairs that the profession has begun to utilize this new tool and explore its full potential.

Currently, then, the use of the computer in student development poses a number of problems: For example, a lag still exists between hardware and software development. Professionals must learn how to manage effectively their new computer resources and how to meet staff training needs in the area of computer literacy. They must also look at new issues of ethics and standards as it becomes apparent that the computer has the potential to harm as well as to help. This sourcebook examines these problems and points to potential solutions.

In addition, this volume provides a broad overview of the software available to the student affairs professional. It aims to give readers a reason for becoming involved with computers and to stimulate their thinking on the many possibilities for computer use.

In Chapter One, K. Richard Pyle presents historical facts about student development and provides a rationale for using the computer to provide the individualized attention that is central to the philosophy of this field. He also cites examples of computer applications that currently exist for career guidance, personal counseling, residence hall management, and work with special populations.

How does one make decisions about which computer to buy in a rapidly changing market? What software programs best meet the needs of a specific student population or match the philosophy of a particular office? Bruce Riesenberg addresses these and other questions in Chapter Two as he offers some useful guidelines for selecting hardware and software.

In Chapter Three, James P. Sampson, Jr., discusses some of

1

the problems that can be created by the computer for the student affairs manager, and he proposes a model for effective management of computer resources so that these problems can be avoided.

In Chapter Four, the cumulative experience of the last two decades of computer application in career guidance is reviewed by Cynthia S. Johnson as an example of how students can benefit by direct access to the computer.

The next chapter offers advice on general purpose software. L. Russell Watjen discusses applications such as electronic spread sheets, data bases, and electronic slide shows that can prove useful to the student affairs manager. These applications not only may free the professional from repetitive tasks but also may expand his or her resources in ways never before possible.

While the computer has the potential to help, it also has the potential to harm. No ethical code or operational standard has yet been developed for computer-assisted student development programs. In the chapter on ethical considerations, James P. Sampson, Jr., discusses potential abuses in the areas of confidentiality, counselor intervention, and testing and assessment.

In the final chapter, K. Richard Pyle describes possibilities for the future as student affairs embraces computer technology and as student development software becomes more plentiful and sophisticated.

Little literature exists in the student affairs field to help a manager or practitioner explore the use of the computer in student development. Professional associations such as the National Association of Student Personal Administrators (NASPA) and the American College Personnel Association (ACPA) are just beginning to offer workshops on the use of computers. Few graduate training programs provide future professionals with computer competency. Research on the effectiveness of student development computer programs is only recently emerging, and as yet no software reviews are appearing in professional journals to guide one in decision making. This volume addresses these problems and calls for further research and information.

The computer has the potential to interact with an individual student and thus to individualize that student's growth toward becoming a fully mature person. Student development educators, then, may finally have a tool to help them accomplish their task. This and other potential uses of this tool have not yet been fully realized, and there is a danger that they never will be if the profession treats the computer as another fad or uses it only as a management tool.

The contributors to this volume have attempted to answer some questions and have raised new ones about the potential of the computer in student development. The authors are all pioneers in the application of computers to student affairs and have managed, counseled, researched, and written about their experiences. In this volume, they share their thoughts and knowledge in the hope that they may demystify the technology and help their colleagues on their journey into the technological age.

Cynthia S. Johnson
K. Richard Pyle
Editors

Cynthia S. Johnson is an assistant professor and cochairperson of the doctoral program in Counseling and Personnel Services, College of Education, University of Maryland, where her courses include one on microcomputers and student affairs. She is currently director of counselor training in the use of technology for adult learners for Project LEARN.

K. Richard Pyle is a counseling psychologist at the University of Texas and has management responsibilities for the career services center. He is currently the associate director of the counselor training component of Project LEARN.

*The computer is particularly well suited to assist the student
development educator in accomplishing the goals of the
profession. A look at current student development applications
provides an idea of the range of possibilities for computer use.*

Computers and Student Development: What Are the Possibilities?

K. Richard Pyle

A Rationale for Computer Use

Student development is a concept that is grounded in the American
belief in the worth of the individual, in the right of the individual to
strive for development to his or her full potential, and in the
individual's right to receive help in reaching that potential. From the
beginning of the guidance and counseling movement (Patterson, 1938;
American Council on Education, 1937), student services professionals
have adopted an orientation that emphasizes responding to the whole
person, attending to individual differences, and working with students
at their current level of development. This emphasis on individual
worth and development was already reflected in the educational process, but it was left to the guidance/student services/student development movement to focus on the concept of individualization. Thus, the
approach at the core of student devclopment recognizes that people
have different needs, values, circumstances, backgrounds, preferences,
plans, developmental rates and styles, and that these differences affect

C. S. Johnson, K. R. Pyle (Eds.). *Enhancing Student Development with Computers.*
New Directions for Student Services, no. 26. San Francisco: Jossey-Bass, June 1984.

the options that are available to them, the choices they make, and the processes by which they make decisions (Katz and Shatkin, 1980).

To cope with such differences and the corresponding need for flexible, individualized treatment, the student development field has depended heavily on having manageable ratios of professional counselors and student development educators to students. Standards for these ratios have been developed by states and professional associations, but, despite heavy funding efforts by federal and state government to improve and support these ratios, the need for greater individualization continues. The recent report of the National Commission on Excellence in Education (1983), which offers a bleak diagnosis of the state of American schools and colleges, demonstrates that more must be done to educate our students effectively — that is, to provide education that keeps up with the needs of our society and the competition from other nations. The commission reports, for example, that "our once unchallenged preeminence in commerce, industry, science, and technological innovation is being overtaken by competitors throughout the world" (p. 6).

How can student development educators go about providing the quality of education and individualization necessary to help students reach their potential? What approaches are needed to facilitate human development more effectively?

American technological ingenuity has provided us a means by which high levels of individualization in education can occur: the computer. Just as the mass production and distribution of automobiles accommodated individual scheduling and transportation needs, computers provide a resource that is attentive to individual differences and responsive to distinctive needs (Katz and Shatkin, 1980). The computer fully attends to the individual with no biases or prejudices. Harris-Bowlsbey (1983) describes this capability for personalization as one of the computer's major advantages: "A system might conceivably administer an instrument to assess career maturity at first sign-on. Then, based upon the scores made on the scales of this instrument, the computer (because of a creative developer's prior work) might deliver quite different levels of readiness for making career decisions. Furthermore, different individuals can receive quite different interpretations of an interest inventory based upon the strength or lack of strength of the profile" (p. 7).

Harris-Bowlsbey lists four other capabilities besides individualization that the computer offers to the student:

1. The computer arouses awareness of the need to plan. Several studies have demonstrated that the use of a computer-assisted

guidance system does effect significant increases in measures of career maturity (Pyle and Stripling, 1976; Super and others, 1981).

2. The computer provides broad awareness of alternatives. The capacity of the computer to store large files of alternatives allows for a vast network of information on a variety of variables. For example, a user can search occupational alternatives by Holland codes, by United States Office of Education (USOE) career clusters, by Roe groups, by American College Testing (ACT) World-of-Work map regions, and so on, in each case accessing the same data file. By integrating and linking a videodisc and player to the computer, the educator makes this function of searching and studying alternatives even more powerful.

3. The computer teaches a process of decision making. The process by which the individual moves through the computer system can be internalized and learned as a decision-making tool. The student accomplishes this indirect learning simply by using the system and following the directions. Tiedeman (1970) describes the computer as a technological "prosthetic device" in support of decision making. More recent research on computer-based systems, however, indicates that the decision-making skill is not easily learned and that long-term computer use is necessary before the student demonstrates significant progress in this skill.

4. The computer provides recent, easily accessible information. This capability is critical for students if they are to be able to compete in the "information age." The computer can access increasingly large amounts of information in nano seconds; it is now a relatively simple process to make information of all kinds available to students. Such a tool frees the student development educator from having to have vast amounts of data and information memorized or in a library of books and periodicals.

Uses of the Computer in Student Development

Early Applications. Computers have historically contributed to such administrative activities as record keeping and data processing. In the 1960s, educators began to explore using computers in developmental activities that centered around career guidance. Leaders in these pioneering efforts were Joseph Impelleteri, David Tiedeman, Donald Super, Frank Minor, Robert Campbell, JoAnn Harris-Bowlsbey, and Martin Katz. The work of these individuals resulted in a number of the presently available computer-assisted guidance programs. Harris-Bowlsbey initially developed and worked with the Computerized Vocational Information System (CVIS) and later DISCOVER. Katz developed the System for Interactive Guidance and Information (SIGI), and Tiedeman developed the Information System for Vocational Decision (ISVD). Donald Super, with Frank Minor of International Business Machines (IBM), designed the Educational and Career Exploration System (ECES). These systems are described in detail in Chapter Four.

Since 1975, when the Employment and Training Administration established a grants program to fund occupational information systems in eight states, there has been a movement to develop state systems. Most states now have or are in the process of putting into place a computerized career information program.

Although administrative tasks and career guidance were the first areas to receive computer assistance, computers are and can be used in all areas of student development. Computers can complement or supplement student development educators, and they can even substitute for them by freeing them from routine information acquisition and exchange. The following subsections look at more of these recent examples of computer use.

Counseling. Computers enable counselors to focus on organizing an individualized learning program for clients; they help counselors gather information, interact with key figures in the client's milieu, and acquire more data by which to evaluate counseling and to serve more clients. In addition, they enable clients to review elements of counseling without consuming counselor time, yet clients still receive feedback congruent with the counselor's plan.

Computer-assisted personal counseling is generally designed to assist individuals in solving personal problems. These systems are used either with the counselor (as part of the counseling process) or without counselor intervention (as an independent, client-controlled resource). The specific purpose and design of existing systems vary considerably according to the therapeutic orientation of the developer. For example, the system developed by Weizenbaum (1965) was based on a client-centered approach, and the systems developed by Colby, Watt, and Gilbert (1966) and Taylor (1970) were based on a psychoanalytic approach. All of these systems were designed more for demonstration purposes than to provide a complete computer-assisted counseling system. In contrast, one of the early complete systems, developed by Greist (1973), evaluated an individual's clinical state and his or her potential for attempting suicide.

The most comprehensive computer-assisted personal counseling system to date was developed by Wagman and Kerber (1980). It is called PLATO Digital Counseling System (DCS), and it operates from a theoretical framework that models the logic pattern of the computer. The system is designed to assist in resolving personal dilemmas by having the client progress through the following four sequenced and interrelated processes: "(a) formulating the original case problem as a psychological dilemma, (b) formulating the creative inquiry for each extraction route, (c) generating solutions for each creative inquiry, and (d) ranking and evaluating solutions" (p. 18). Individuals are referred to PLATO DCS by a counselor, or they can request the use of the system. Follow-up counseling is available if requested by the individual.

Therapists are also developing ways to use the computer as an aid in the therapy process. An example of this is a program developed by Clark and Schroech (1983), who designed a computer therapeutic game to provide support and advice to adolescents without causing anger and resentment. The game provides incentives for attending therapy, removes the stigma typically associated with the concept of self-control, and replaces it with interest in attaining self-control. Using a game format similar to Dungeons and Adventure (Adams, 1980), the developers have designed a software system that helps clients become more cooperative and enthusiastic about treatment. Clients discuss problem behavior in light of the game without becoming resistant to therapy. Clark and Schroech state that "as computers are increasingly used in the therapeutic process, traditional therapeutic underpinnings will be replaced by concepts we have yet to discover" (p. 19).

The counseling center at Michigan State University has put a computer to use in its self-management laboratory (SML) to counsel students on study habits, time management, test anxiety, career choice, and personal problem solving. Through the use of two SML terminals or by telephone connections to personal computers or other campus terminals, students can access the self-management system. Following simple instructions printed on the terminal screen, they can give or receive messages from others, reach a file describing how to utilize campus facilities, or look at one of two self-help programs: skill development and information resources. The self-help programs are broken down into topics, and the topics are further broken down into specific categories. Some programs are informative, and others are interactive, with computer responses based on student answers to questions. The progression from the main list of files to more specific topics is simple. The computer always provides instructions on how to proceed or return to the start.

Under test taking, for example, a student can acquire a list of general remarks or a systematic breakdown of what to do the night before, the morning of, and during a test. The advice in each step is specific: don't guzzle coffee to stay awake; avoid personal disagreements just before a test; take candy with you to an exam. Gordon Williams, who developed the SML and its computer systems, explains that a self-help approach is both a supplement to regular one-to-one counseling and a way of reaching students who need help but won't seek personal counseling.

Academic Advising. It is interesting to note that, as computers have increased in use in the past five years, so have the interest in and recognition of the value of academic advising. In 1979 the National Academic Advising Association (NACADA) was established. Since then, NACADA has gained a large membership and set up annual conferences as well as its own professional journal. With the parallel newness and growth of advising and computers, it is not surprising that computers are being used heavily by a number of institutions in order to keep students and advisers informed on the complexities of curricular course sequencing, degree options, and graduation requirements.

Computer-assisted advising programs operate on the principle of matching degree requirements with student academic records. Reports are produced that show graduation requirements and the progress of the student in completing these requirements. In addition, the reports can include the student's course record, individual requirements, waivers or substitutions, additional credit gained (for example, from advanced placement, the College Level Examination Program, or the military), a statement of proficiency in completing the requirements, and whom to see and where to go for additional assistance (Spencer and others, 1982).

A number of institutions are using the computer in unique and innovative ways (Kramer and others, 1983). The University of Denver, for example, has developed a simple, efficient, and cost-effective advising report system. By batch-processing the data once a semester and storing the data on computer tapes, the system makes information on students' progress readily available to advisers. The system was developed inexpensively and costs approximately two cents per progress report printed.

Purdue University has developed a unique progress report design. On one page it includes thirty-five segments of information, including a matrix that plots the degree requirements for the eight semesters of the baccalaureate program. In each box of the matrix, the department name and the number of the required course is shown. For each student, the system prints the earned grade, semester and year taken, and number of credit hours accumulated in the box corresponding to the course.

North Carolina State University designed its automated degree audit system as a centralized system with decentralized decision making and data loading. There are nine schools and eighty departments in the university; each department and school is responsible for coding and entering its own information.

Georgia State University's advisement and degree auditing system is not only one of the oldest advising systems but it is also the only transportable system that is sold to other universities. Most degree audit systems are designed for a particular institution's environment. The Georgia State Programmed Academic Curriculum Evaluation (PACE) system has been implemented successfully at several other colleges and universities.

Brigham Young University's system is unique for its completely on line computer capabilities as one segment of a larger student information system. It uses a data base approach, so that advisers can access degree files and student academic records of student progress.

Miami-Dade Community College has an expanded approach to advising. Academic advising is supported through three systems. The Advisement and Graduation Information System (AGIS) goes beyond degree tracking to include on line computer access to lists of the courses (by degree program) offered at Florida's colleges and universities that are recommended for a special transfer-by-degree program. The Academic Alert System is used early in the semester to identify both students who have academic difficulty and those who are outstanding students. The system generates either early-warning letters or letters of encouragement. The third support system, the Standards of Academic Progress, is used at the end of the semester to identify students who have weak academic records.

Research evidence exists that lends support to the use of computers in advising: Aitken and Conrad (1977) found that the computerized academic progress report was the significant factor in reducing errors in advising and in improving academic advising for degree requirements. Vitelli and Singleton (1972) reported that students were much more confident about information provided them on the "computer run" than they were with the old system of contacting faculty members about proper requirements, required prerequisites, and the correct sequence of courses. Evidence exists that advising with a computerized graduation checklist is cost-justified, reducing previous costs by one quarter (Sego and Unger, 1977). Spencer and others (1982) indicate that "the benefits of a computer-based advisement system can be summed up in five key words: speed, accuracy, ease, frequency, and cost" (pp. 176–177).

Study Skills/Tutoring. William F. Brown of Texas Southwestern

University and James Sampson of Florida State University have developed study skills programs. Their programs, although arranged in different sequence, basically assist the student to improve in a variety of study skills areas. These areas include managing time, improving memory and motivation, reading textbooks, taking lecture notes, and improving concentration. In addition to these, a program developed by Instructional Enterprises of Madison, Wisconsin, helps students through assessing their learning styles and thought processes and evaluating the implications of each style for studying and attitude development.

A number of tutoring programs are now available through software companies. These range from assistance with a particular subject area to help in preparing for the Graduate Record Examination (GRE). Optimized Systems Software of Cupertino, California, has developed a speed-reading tutor that trains users to recognize recurring words and phrases. It can be used as part of a self-study tutorial or as a teaching aid when used in conjunction with college texts.

Testing. Testing companies have been quick to adapt tests for the computer. Many counseling and career centers now provide students with an opportunity for on line testing. Florida State has developed testing systems for handicapped students that allow the student to complete a particular test, including its interpretation, no matter what their handicap. In addition, it is possible for students to take the Myers-Briggs Personality Type Indicator on line and have their scores interpreted through a video monitor.

As a consequence of a test authoring program developed by James Lee of Instructional Enterprises, educators can put any of their favorite tests on the computer without having to know how to program. The authoring program writes the test program after the directions are typed in. Similarly, the educator can now prepare a training/tutoring/testing device for students without having to do the basic programming. The educator enters instructions and information, which are then keyed to a tutorial drill or test. The user may choose between a multiple-choice, fill-in-the-blank, or column-match test format. This program has been developed by Micro Lay of Highland Park, Illinois.

Registration. At such diverse schools as Prince Georges Community College in Maryland and the University of Texas at Austin, registration depends heavily on the computer. Using a system modeled on one used by the airlines, students can telephone in or walk to a terminal, order a class, be told if seats are available, and receive immediate confirmation. The computer then generates a bill and activates an information system that automatically adjusts the financial aid award, adjusts the counselor's file on credit toward graduation, and if appropriate, notifies the Veterans Administration office.

It is indeed unusual to find any institution that does not use the computer in some way for registration. This is one area that easily lends itself to computer application.

Placement. Placement personnel have discovered a number of uses for the computer (Bruce and others, 1982). Boston University placement staff, for example, have developed the Computerized Scheduling Program (CSP), which selects students on the basis of credentials and then schedules interviews. Students complete an optical-scan input sheet with each resumé submitted for consideration by an on-campus recruiter. The computer can scan this input at the rate of thousands of forms an hour.

A resumé retrieval program, which is a function of the microcomputer and word processor, has also been developed. The data bank contains a file, or a minidescription, on each student using the placement office. Companies requesting specific criteria when determining their needs for a position are easily matched with a list of possible candidates. For example, the computer might list all Spanish-speaking marketing majors or all finance majors seeking employment with an international banking institution.

The Job Opportunity Bank (JOB) is a computerized data bank of employment opportunities for students and alumni. An ongoing file records past openings and maintains a contact list of all employers who have filed jobs with the office. The system is capable of matching professional interests, geographic preference, and salary range with the positions in the data bank.

The Career Placement Registry (CPR) offers potential employers access to the credentials of qualified seniors and graduate students on file in the system. Employers can search the data base on all of the following criteria: college, degree, major and minor, grades, career preferences, geographic preferences, spatial skills, relevant experience, and so forth. Such a system can be an effective resource both for students looking for unusual job opportunities and for employers who do not recruit on campus. Students can market themselves to employers in many geographic areas, both nationally and internationally (Bruce and others, 1982).

A number of interactive computer programs have been developed to aid students in their resumé development and job search. These programs use accepted career development principles to give students a basic understanding of what goes into a good resumé and of how to find a position (Blakeley and Johnson, 1983).

Financial Aid. The large amount of data and the need to integrate and synthesize information make financial aid well suited for computer application. Today it is unusual to find an institution that does not use the computer in the financial aid process. In particular, the computer is very helpful in three major financial aid areas: needs analysis and assessment to determine the level of student need; the packaging process that determines the portion of assistance from grants, loans, and college work study to be made available to each student; and loan follow-up, which is required to meet the federal guidelines of due diligence. Among other areas in which the computer has been helpful is in determining a typical budget necessary for students to go to school. From such basic information, an institution is able to determine a base line for their financial aid program.

Program Evaluation and Research. The use of computers as a tool in program evaluation is proving invaluable to institutions that want to develop more accountability and are interested in determining the impact of their student development efforts. The computer has the capacity to store vast amounts of student data that can be extracted and studied with ease. Consequently, institutions are developing data bases that can be used for the purposes of research and accountability.

At the University of Texas, longitudinal data files have been developed to help answer retention questions. These systems determine the relationship of retention to student participation in a particular program (such as study skills workshops and leadership retreats). In addition, such a data base helps to determine what forms, if any, of financial aid tend to help retain students.

Alma College in Michigan uses a data base to provide information on the level of job-search confidence that graduating students have as they enter the job market. Such data is invaluable in helping to justify the college's career preparation program and in the recruitment of new students. The data base provides the opportunity to look at the impact of a variety of career preparation activities and events.

A number of student development departments use data bases as a means of communicating to colleges and faculty departments the unique characteristics of their entering students. These profiles include such indexes as Scholastic Aptitude Test (SAT) scores, educational aspirations, past grades, and social, educational, and academic needs and beliefs.

The easy generation and access to such large amounts of data heightens the interest in and feasibility of research. For example, computer-assisted guidance programs such as SIGI can provide the researcher with a window to see how students go about making decisions by allowing the researcher to track the process by which students go through the system itself.

It is commonplace now to use the computer to help us with the assessment of data and with the application of statistical methodology to a set of data. Such use makes the research effort less cumbersome and more efficient.

Career Development/Decision Making. Career guidance was one of the first areas where computers were applied to student development. Consequently, a host of programs have evolved and are now on the market. Chief among these are DISCOVER, SIGI, Guidance Information System (GIS), Career Information System (CIS), Computerized Heuristic Occupational Information and Career Exploration System (CHOICES), EUREKA, and the Coordinated Occupational Information Network (COIN). (See Chapter Four for further descriptions of these systems.) SIGI and DISCOVER are considered to be "guidance" systems since they not only provide information but also serve a planning and synthesis function that helps the user to apply information to decisions (Katz and Shatkin, 1980). The other systems focus primarily on giving information with the expectation that the counselor will play a major role in the synthesis of the information. (This does not mean that the developers of SIGI and DISCOVER intend for their systems to stand alone.)

New programs assist students in the development of decision-making skills. A program developed by Lemire and Cox (in press) called FATE (Formulating Alternatives to Enhance Experience) helps the user to work through a decision systematically. A related program, directed at both decision making and leadership development, in called Outdoor Education Computer Simulation by Lemire and Cox. This program uses the aptitudes needed in leading groups in wilderness survival to assist in the development of leadership and decision-making skills.

Several student development educators have integrated the computer into an ongoing teaching/counseling process. Alma College, for example, uses a computer-assisted guidance program (SIGI) as part of a laboratory experience within their career preparation modules and group career counseling programs. Moraine Valley Community College in Illinois and the University of Texas Career Center follow a similar laboratory approach with DISCOVER and their career development classes and groups.

Special Populations. Computers are providing individual assistance to special populations. For example, programs have been developed in which the print is oversized for the partially sighted and/or have voice synthesizers attached to the computer. The National Institute for the Deaf has found computer-assisted guidance programs particularly beneficial (Johnson, 1983). Since the computer treats all people the same, people who have been susceptible to bias in the past can now receive information relatively free of prejudice. In addition, there are always students who feel more comfortable accessing information in the privacy of a computer carrel rather than with a counselor.

With the help of a W. K. Kellogg grant, researchers are developing special computer programs to assist adults in making the transition from work to education. Both the Educational Testing Service and the American College Testing Program are developing adult versions of SIGI and DISCOVER. The program will assist adults in (1) assessing the roles they have played in life, (2) determining the skills gained through work experience, (3) developing a portfolio of prior experience that can be used for potential college credit, and (4) accessing career information and college information. Videodiscs, connected to the computer, enable the adult learner to view the work place or actually see a campus. Additional programs modules for adults are being developed by Arthur Chickering at Memphis State University. These modules focus on learning styles, adult development, and life cycle and are intended to expand self-awareness and broaden perspectives for career and educational planning.

Residence Halls/Student Activities. In residence halls, student development educators find computers to be helpful in roommate pairing, housekeeping activities, record keeping, and providing up-to-date information about the campus and services. In the student activities area, computers have been used creatively in social matches, needs assessment, and programming activities.

A pilot project at the University of Wisconsin–Stevens Point that has both student activity and career development potential is entitled Total Involvement Educational System (TIES). The program is a comprehensive computerized network designed to integrate experiential learning opportunities and human development efforts with the traditional education milieu (Moffat, 1983).

TIES operates from a data base consisting of precise descriptions for each complementary experience available at the University of Wisconsin–Stevens Point. The categories for these complementary experiences are: practicum/field work, volunteer/service-learning positions, student organization positions, performing activities (such as fine arts performing groups or athletics), paid student employment positions (both on and off campus), scholarships and awards, and discrete training opportunities. All positions are described by type, skills involved, links to the world of work, and relevance to the university curriculum.

Students use TIES through an interactive program on a computer terminal. After signing on at the terminal, each student user is introduced to the concept of using information systems to select complementary activities and is then asked a series of questions to assist the computer program in being responsive to individual needs. For example, the interactive program will request the student's collegiate level and academic major.

The components of TIES's interactive computer program are as follows:

1. Guiding—In this section, students are provided with information about the purpose of the system and are then invited to conduct self-assessments to define their specific reasons for using TIES. For example, students may choose specific skills that they want to develop through extracurricular experiences.

2. Understanding—In this part of the program, TIES defines various types of skills such as functional, self-management, and work-specific skills. In addition, the system explains how these skills can emerge both through academic studies and through involvement in the extracurriculum and how these skills are applied in the world of work.

3. Investigating—In this section, the student begins to make choices for involvement by selecting from a menu of complementary activities. The student user refers to his or her own self-assessment from the first two sections of TIES to select a frame of reference for investigating complementary activities. Then the information system displays descriptions for any position that the student user might select.

4. Doing—This section directs the student user to the specific people and material resources to pursue a specific complementary activity further. An optional segment of this section teaches the student how to interview for information.

5. Evaluating—In this section, a student has an opportunity to build and review a personal Student Involvement Record, which records for each student the full range of completed complementary activities in a personalized resumé-type format.

Some of the major goals of TIES are: (1) to teach students to articulate their skills, (2) to allow students to choose extracurricular learning opportunities in a systematic fashion, (3) to allow students to investigate career directions through both course work and experiences outside the classroom, and (4) to centralize existing information sources and provide a more readily accessible encyclopedia of complementary experiences for students.

Telecomputing and Student Development

The marriage of the computer and the telephone offers student development educators a rich resource. Called *telecomputing,* this is one of the fastest growing uses for personal computers. It is also an area where a spirit of cooperation and even altruism flourishes in the midst of a highly competitive industry.

For educators, connecting the computer to the telephone opens up an efficient and inexpensive channel of communication. Educators may find it a way to improve the quality of information available for decision making, while holding down communication costs. A page of double-spaced text can be sent from one computer to another in the United States over an ordinary telephone circuit in about thirteen seconds. A 100-page report takes about twenty minutes. After a document has been transmitted in this manner, any number of copies in a variety of formats can be printed at the receiving end.

Because of its speed and accuracy, telecomputing is often superior to the mail and to ordinary telephone calls for sending detailed information. Except where graphics are involved, telecomputing usually is faster and provides better copy than telephone-fascimile machines.

For the data exchange by telephone, the computer is equipped with a piece of equipment called a *modem.* This device converts into sound the on-and-off electrical pulses that the computer uses internally. These sounds are transmitted over a telephone circuit.

Presently, there are three major ways by which personal computer users exchange information over the telephone network. The first is the exchange of general information on a variety of topics that takes the form of a bulletin board. This approach allows the users to communicate information to one another and to extract information from a host of data bases. The second use is in the exchange of information on the latest computer software. The third is the actual exchange of the software program so that it can be used on one's own computer.

The bulletin board opens up many potential applications for the student development professional. Once a bulletin board is dialed, it transmits messages left by other users to one's computer and accepts new messages. Consequently, bulletin board applications offer educators a way to communicate with each other, either by leaving a message to a specific user or by broadcasting a public message to everyone who logs into the bulletin board. Telecomputing also allows the student development educator to access clearinghouses directly to receive such data as the most up-to-date research information and information on new and innovative programs. In addition, the opportunity exists to solve problems with the help of other professionals in an efficient and economical manner. Such activity often takes place at conferences and conventions; now it can take place via the telephone. Finally, this resource provides the opportunity to keep one's computer software programs at the state of the art through the ease of exchange.

Computer services of this kind are still in their infancy. The technology that allows computers to disseminate information is already well developed, but the potential for applying this technology for business and institutional use has barely been tapped. Presently, experiments are taking place to establish nationwide computer networks that will permit users to book airline or hotel reservations, make purchases from electronic catalogues, pay bills, and conduct banking transactions with personal computers. The marriage of the computer and the telephone enormously extends the capacity of each constituent technology for communication, information transfer, and commerce. It is no longer a matter of whether this potential will be developed, it is only a matter of when and to what extent.

Summary

The value of and need for individual attention in the human development learning process is a cardinal value of American higher education. This chapter describes the individualizing potential of the computer as well as a cross section of student development functions and computer applications. Although research is still limited as to the impact of computer programs on student growth, it appears that computers have the potential to enhance student learning. The extent of that potential will depend upon the student development educators' interest and motivation to use this new tool appropriately.

References

Adams, S. "Pirates' Adventures." *BYTE,* January 1980, *5* (1), 192–212.

Aitken, C. E., and Conrad, C. F. "Improving Academic Advising Through Computerization." *College and University,* 1977, *53,* 115–123.

American Council on Education. *The Student Personnel Point of View.* American Council on Education Studies, Series 1, *1* (3). Washington, D.C.: American Council on Education, 1937.

Blakeley, J., and Johnson, C. S. "Software Clearinghouse for Student Services: Software and Resource Catalogue." Unpublished paper, March 1983.

Bruce, B., Shuman, R., and Varelas, E. "Technology in Career Planning and Placement." *Journal of College Placement,* Summer 1982, 31–32.

Clark, E., and Schroech, K. "A Computer-Assisted Therapeutic Game for Adolescents." *Computers in Psychiatry/Psychology,* 1983, *5* (3), 34–39.

Colby, K. M., Watt, J. F., and Gilbert, J. P. "A Computer Method of Psychotherapy's Preliminary Communication." *Journal of Nervous and Mental Diseases,* 1966, 142–148.

Greist, N. J. "A Computer Interview for Suicide-Risk Prediction." *American Journal of Psychiatry,* 1973, *130,* 1327–1332.

Harris-Bowlsbey, J. "A Historical Perspective." In C. Johnson (Ed.), *Microcomputers and the School Counselor.* Alexandria, Va.: American School Counselor Association, 1983.

Johnson, C. (Ed.). *Microcomputers and the School Counselor.* Alexandria, Va.: American School Counselor Association, 1983.

Katz, M. R., and Shatkin, L. *Computer-Assisted Guidance: Concepts and Practices.* Princeton, N.J.: Educational Testing Service, 1980.

Kramer, G. L., Peterson, E. D., and Spencer, R. W. "Utilization of Computers in Academic Advising." Unpublished paper, Brigham Young University, October 1983.

Lemire, D., and Cox, S. "The Outdoor Experiential Simulation: A Conceptual Model and Rationale." *The Small School Forum* (in press).

Moffat, N. "A Pilot Project to Assess Student Development Through Extraclass Activities." Unpublished paper, University of Wisconsin, 1983.

National Commission on Excellence in Education. "Our Nation Is at Risk." *Chronicle of Higher Education,* 1983, *26* (10), 1–6.

Patterson, D. G. "The Genesis of Modern Guidance." *Educational Record,* 1938, *19,* 36–46.

Pyle, K. R., and Stripling, R. O. "The Counselor, the Computer, and Career Development." *Vocational Guidance Quarterly,* 1976, *25,* 71–76.

Sego, R. J., and Unger, E. A. "The Computer to the Rescue." *Journal of Home Economics,* 1977, *69,* 55–57.

Spencer, R. W., Peterson, E. D., Nielsen, R. B., and Kramer, G. L. "Advisement by Computer (ABC): A Tool for Improving Academic Advising." *College and University,* 1982, *57,* 169–179.

Super, D. E., Lindeman, R. H., Thomas, A. S., Myers, R. A., and Jordan, J. P. *Career Development Inventory.* Palo Alto, Calif.: Consulting Psychologists Press, 1981.

Taylor, K. *Computer Applications in Psychotherapy: Bibliography and Abstracts* (PHS No. 1981). Washington, D.C.: U.S. Government Printing Office, 1970.

Tiedeman, D. V. *Third Report: Information System for Vocational Decisions.* Cambridge, Mass.: Harvard Graduate School of Education, 1970.

Vitelli, R. A., and Singleton, R. L. "Computer-Assisted Advising and Degree Evaluation." *College and University,* 1972, *47,* 494–502.

Wagman, M., and Kerber, K. W. "PLATO DCS, An Interactive Computer System for Personal Counseling: Further Development and Evaluation." *Journal of Counseling Psychology,* 1980, *27,* 31–34.

Weizenbaum, J. "ELIZA: A Computer Program for the Study of Natural Language Communication Between Man and Machine." *Communications of the Association for Computing Machinery,* 1965, *9,* 36–45.

K. Richard Pyle is a counseling psychologist at the University of Texas and has management responsibilities for the career services center. He is currently the associate director of the counselor training component of Project LEARN.

The key to the selection of computer hardware and software
for student development applications is a thorough and
systematic analysis of needs and expectations.

Selecting Computer Hardware and Software

Bruce Riesenberg

Where to Begin: The Problem Definition

Selecting computer hardware and software can be a nightmare if you have not defined your needs, the problems you want to solve with the computer, and your priorities for its use in your operating unit or in the overall student development division. Engaging in this definition process may take time and a lot of hard thought, but it is absolutely necessary if your purchase is going to be successful. In the words of one computer expert (Grosswirth, 1983), "The current consensus is to (1) determine what your needs are; (2) determine what software is already available to satisfy those needs; and (3) buy the computer that within those constraints of your budget will best run the software you need to meet your requirements" (p. 139). Figure 1 illustrates a decision-making model to assist with the process suggested by Grosswirth.

Reasons for considering the use of the computer in student development are as diverse as the field of student development itself. This book provides many examples of these varied uses; here we list just a few areas where computer systems can be used effectively:

- To provide career guidance and occupational information
- To teach study skills and test taking

C. S. Johnson, K. R. Pyle (Eds.). *Enhancing Student Development with Computers.*
New Directions for Student Services, no. 26. San Francisco. Jossey-Bass, June 1984.

Figure 1. Decision-Making Model for Selecting Computer Hardware and Software

Step	Task	Questions to Ask
I	Define needs.	What alternatives are there to using the computer to meet your needs?
II	Identify specialized problem areas and requirements.	What are your specialized requirements within the overall area of need? (List those requirements.)
		What budget do you have to work within? What priorities can be cut, given budget restraints?
III	Work with vendors to identify existing software programs and hardware requirements.	What packaged or existing software programs are available that might meet your requirements?
IV	Compare system capabilities with needs.	Evaluate existing software programs against your requirements. Is there a match?
V	Compare systems' features and costs.	Is the necessary hardware available/affordable? Is the necessary funding available?
		Do you have top management support? Do you have staff support?
VI	Determine other users. Get hands-on experience.	Do other users' experiences and your hands-on experience support your preliminary evaluation?
VII	Make purchase or return to Step IV.	

- To schedule programs, events, campus tours, room usage, equipment availability, and recruitment interviews
- For record keeping
- For budget administration
- To maintain accountability data and statistics
- For word processing
- To facilitate inventory control.

Defining needs is probably not too difficult in itself; what may be most time consuming is the determination of specific requirements within each area of need — that is, analyzing your specialized problems and your priorities for resolving them. For example, take the area of career planning and placement: You may have decided to purchase a computer system to assist with career guidance or planning needs. But the decision must go further than that. You must decide, among other things, what you want the system to do. Do you want it simply to provide occupational information, or do you want a guidance or decision-making component? Do you want local or national occupational data? What age group will be the primary user? Does the system need to be portable? How much space do you have? Do you want students to have direct access to the terminal? How much counselor intervention time do you have available? How often will the equipment be used? What is your current guidance philosophy?

Another example lies in the area of student union management. You may have decided you want a computer system to assist with room scheduling for various organizations' events. But are there other uses for which a computer system would be helpful? For instance, could you also use it for inventory control, for maintaining a data base for procedures reports on room set-up, for an automated billing system, and for word processing? There are systems currently available that can handle all of these functions (and more) on one piece of equipment.

Perhaps a counseling center has decided to use a computer to track client needs at particular times of the year. But would it be wise to consider a system that also can handle accountability data for budget justification and is the center's budget large enough that a computer system could improve its management?

There are certainly many more examples that could be cited, and you will find many more in the other chapters of this book. But to maximize the effectiveness of the purchase and the choice of both software and hardware, you must first undertake a thorough analysis of existing as well as potential needs. As stated by Hurley, "one of the underlying reasons for the failure of systems to perform to initial expectations is the lack of systematic procedures for acquiring and analyzing user needs and expectations prior to system design and development" (Hurley, 1981, p. 168).

Other considerations to take into account prior to the selection of your system include budget, staff attitudes, the institutional political environment, cost effectiveness (are there alternatives to the purchase of a computer system that may prove to be more easily obtainable at a lower cost?), and budget for staffing and future maintenance of a system. More than one manager has been fired over the purchase of an expensive system that turned out to be inappropriate or unacceptable given the environment and needs.

Determining Software Needs

As the model presented in Figure 1 shows, once a thorough analysis of needs and alternatives has been conducted, the next step is to determine processing requirements for use of the equipment — in computer language, these are the *software* requirements. Depending on identified needs, software requirements will vary widely. Do you require a system that employs the use of graphic displays, and will the graphics be straight lines, images, or circular configurations? Is color important, or is a black and white or green and white screen display sufficient? Should the software program be able to display data as well as information frames on the video screen (called the cathode ray tube or CRT)? How complex are the transactions that will be completed? How large a data base or file capacity will be required?

At this point, a number of solutions are possible. You can select a prepackaged software system that meets your needs, hire a computer programmer or systems analyst to write a program to suit your particular needs, or select a partially programmed software package that can be fully programmed to meet your needs.

Now you need to find out whether packaged software programs are available that will meet your needs or whether a special program must be written for your particular requirements. Several approaches are possible:

1. Contact colleagues in the same area of student development to discuss their experience with computer applications. Did they purchase a software package? How effective is it? Are they pleased with their selection of hardware equipment, or were they given no choice — for instance, the software only runs on one company's hardware, or the equipment needed was already in place and capable of running the program?

2. Engage a consultant to review your software requirements in

2. Engage a consultant to review your software requirements in relation to identified needs. The consultant may also be familiar with the preprogrammed systems available and should be able to determine the feasibility of and costs involved in writing an original program to suit your needs.

3. Visit computer fairs and professional conferences where software programs are demonstrated and discussed. More regional and national conferences (APA, AACD, CPC, Western College Placement Association [WCPA], California Association of College and University Housing Offices [CACUHO], CAEL, and others) are including demonstrations of and workshops on the use of computers in higher education.

4. Visit retail computer stores or call on company representatives to discuss your software needs in relation to their products. (You will, of course, be getting the sales pitch at the same time, so be prepared with the pertinent questions you want answered.)

5. Write for company brochures and catalogues describing computer software programs and the required computer hardware.

Purchasing Packaged Software Programs

If you decide to purchase someone else's software program, several factors need to be considered. First, has the software package been thoroughly tested both in the laboratory and in the field by a variety of users like yourself? Often what sounds good in a brochure or in a sales pitch can be a disappointment once installed. It is important, therefore, to determine how long the package has been in existence, the extent of which it has been tested and "debugged," and, of course, the extent to which it meets your predetermined needs.

Second, will backup be provided if problems develop later with the software; that is, will there be someone available to debug the system if something goes wrong? Is access to the software source code available for purchase with the package? This is particularly important if you are unsure about the quality of software support available or if the manufacturer is distant and hard to reach.

Another consideration is how often the software package is updated, particularly if it contains an information component that is of a changing nature, like labor market trends or occupational information.

Finally, what hardware is it designed to run on? Is it designed for just one company's equipment or for several? Is it available for use on microprocessor equipment, on a minicomputer, on a large mainframe system, or are there several versions available? Do you have the appropriate equipment, or will you need to buy it? What is the cost of the program? Is it a one-time purchase or a yearly lease, and what are the charges for system updates or debugging? Can you get hands-on experience?

At this point, you can use a checklist to evaluate your software purchase (see Figure 2). Rate each system from one to five, five being the highest rating, to summarize and compare the software under consideration.

Computer Hardware Considerations

Your software needs are going to play a large role in the choice of your computer hardware, particularly if you have decided to buy a packaged software program. The more options you have, combined with the extremely rapid changes in available equipment sizes, types, and capabilities, the more complex the task of equipment choice is. If, however, the software program selected is capable of running on existing equipment through the linking of terminals or microcomputers to a mainframe computer (such as a PDP-11), your involvement in actual hardware choice becomes less extensive and may even be predetermined. However, if you purchase your own smaller stand-alone equipment, or it you are involved in the selection of new mainframe equipment (for example, for use in processing vast amounts of administrative data), there are many considerations.

Figure 2. Checklist for Software Selection

Rate systems on a scale from one to five, five being the highest rating.

	Program		
	X	Y	Z
Extent Program Meets Identified Needs	___	___	___
Length of Time on the Market	___	___	___
Probability of Trouble-Free Use	___	___	___
Backup Support Available	___	___	___
Ease of Use	___	___	___
Ease of Learning	___	___	___
Color Capability	___	___	___
Graphics Capability	___	___	___
Size of Data Base or File Capacity	___	___	___
Use of Color/Graphics	___	___	___
Value for Money	___	___	___
Availablity of Hardware Needed	___	___	___
Quality/Reliability of Hardware Needed	___	___	___
Total Point Ratings	___	___	___

As mentioned above, purchase of hardware may be strongly influenced by availability of software, by software requirements, by the existence on campus of equipment, its cost and availability for use, and by the desirability of having several terminals in one office (or terminals in a variety of locations) all connected to one computer. Therefore, researching the existence of currently owned equipment and evaluating that equipment to software requirements is a desirable first step in hardware selection. If your campus is fairly large, you will probably have a central computing facility with personnel available to provide the needed information. The computer center staff may have already been consulted in the determination of your software needs, and, in the process, they may have evaluated those needs for use on existing equipment.

Advantages to the use of existing mainframe equipment include the opportunity to purchase terminals that can also function as stand-alone microprocessors for other purposes, the mainframe's large capacity and storage capabilities, and availability of staff support for debugging and program writing. Disadvantages may arise, however, in the form of charges for computer time and storage space (that is, the storage and maintenance of the software program), down time (because of computer maintenance, multiple users, or overload), and variations in the speed of transmission. For the purposes of this chapter, consideration criteria are directed toward the selection of microcomputers.

Criteria for the Evaluation of Microcomputer Equipment

As we suggested for rating the software being considered, a checklist approach assists with computer hardware comparison. Using the same one-to-five point system, you can evaluate the criteria described in the following paragraphs (see Figure 3).

Choice of Computer Manufacturer. The determination of the brand of computer you buy will be influenced by your software requirements and by the capabilities of the company's product. If you have the choice, the length of the company's existence, its product and service reputation, and the company's strength and financial condition are important considerations. Other considerations are the company's selection of models and its peripheral equipment options, the equipment's compatibility with existing equipment on campus, and the company's distribution methods.

Memory Capacity. Again, the amount of memory required for your computer hardware will be a function of your software needs. For most microcomputers, available memory capacity varies widely; the

Figure 3. Criteria for the Evaluation of Computer Hardware

Rate systems on a scale from one to five, five being the highest rating.

	Computer		
	X	Y	Z
Reputation of Computer Manufacturer	____	____	____
Memory Capacity	____	____	____
Expansion Capabilities	____	____	____
Software Available Meets Needs	____	____	____
Multiple Display Terminals	____	____	____
Other Expansion Options	____	____	____
Video Display	____	____	____
Printers	____	____	____
Keyboards	____	____	____
Networking	____	____	____
Hardware Support	____	____	____
Training and Documentation	____	____	____
Color/Graphics Capability	____	____	____
Value for Money	____	____	____
Total Point Ratings	____	____	____

major criterion is that it be large enough to run the desired software program or programs. Also an important consideration is the ability to expand the system's memory capacity for future needs. Most systems are designed so that memory can be expanded through the addition of circuits to the existing equipment.

Expansion Capabilities. In addition to memory, there are a number of other things that can be expanded to meet future needs. These include:

Storage Capacity. The most frequently used method of information storage on microcomputers is disc storage. The most popular sizes are either five-and-one-quarter-inch or eight-inch discs. The discs are inserted in the machine and read by the disc drive unit in a manner similar to the operation of a record player. The two most frequently used types of discs are soft (or "floppy") and hard. These discs and the equipment used to run them determine the storage capacity of the system. Storage capacity will be determined by the software program desired and can be increased on most systems through the addition of discs running on disc drive expansion units or through the addition of hard disc capability. Although more expensive, the hard disc is faster and stores more information than the soft disc.

Multiple Display Terminals. If future needs may require that display terminals and printers be placed in more than one location, it is important to determine if additional units can be added to the main microcomputer. It is also important to know whether the additional terminals will be able to process multiple tasks at the same time. Another consideration might be the system's ability to add monitors to handle color or graphic displays, if such features might be required by the purchase of new software in the future.

Other Expansion Options. Although it may be difficult to predict future expansion needs when making your initial purchase, the more options available, the more flexible is the system. Other options may include the addition of communications modems to link your microcomputer to a central mainframe system, the range of size and type of printers the system will handle, and the addition of equipment that will allow the system to handle more than one computer language as new software becomes available.

Video Display. Most microcomputers designed for businesses or educational institutions are used primarily with television-like monitors called cathode ray tubes or CRTs. The CRTs are either attached to the computer itself of connected by cable. Some manufacturers produce equipment that can be connected to standard television sets, as can many of the personal computers designed for home use. In general, because of a lower quality of picture clarity and sharpness of imagery, television sets are less favorable for use with the kind of software programs that you will be considering for an institutional setting.

Video display units also differ in size of display or number of characters per line on the screen. Most microcomputers have from forty to eighty characters per line, called either a forty-column or an eighty-column screen. For most software needs, the eighty-column screen is preferable. This option also affects the size of the screen necessary for viewing. If your software needs an eighty-column screen, a twelve-, fifteen-, or nineteen-inch screen is preferable.

Another consideration is the need for color or color graphic displays. If color or color graphics are not considerations, a monochrome (usually black and white or green and white) monitor is sufficient and less costly. Again, however, the consideration of future software needs may warrant the selection of color and color graphic display monitors even though they may not be needed at present.

Printers. Printers are used to produce hard copy of video displays and are connected to the computer unit by cable. For some software programs, such as those used with word-processing systems, the printer is a necessity. For other programs, it may be preferable to have hard copy capability, or it may be left to the user's option. Printers vary in size, print speed, type style and size of print, quality of print, and in noise level. Your printing needs, of course, depend on the use of the printed copy; for example, you need a letter-quality printer if you will be using the computer for word-processing.

The least expensive printers are called thermal or dot-matrix printers. Letter-quality printers, usually called daisy-wheel printers (because they use a ball element to print), are more expensive and require a longer time to print copy. Other variations include width of the print page, graphics capabilities, and the method of connection to the computer.

Printers vary widely in price and capability, so consider your needs carefully. Also, most microcomputer equipment is designed to handle more than one type of printer. Therefore, you may choose to buy a less expensive model at first and upgrade the system later for word-processing needs or to meet the requirements of new software programs.

Keyboards. Typewriter-like keyboards are used to enable user contact with the microcomputer. Keyboards vary in durability, feel (or "touch"), and in the overall configuration of the keys. The feel or touch of the keyboard becomes more important the more time you will be spending in direct communication with your computer. Durability becomes more important with the degree of keyboard use and with the number of different users of the equipment.

Another factor to consider in the selection of the keyboard (in the case of many models the keyboard is attached directly to the computer, so the choice goes with the choice of equipment itself) is the presence of a numeric key pad. This is a section of keys numbered and configured like a calculator board and is important if any kind of accounting or bookkeeping will be done or if the use of a numerical data bank is planned.

Networking. Networking refers to the ability to communicate from one computer to another computer program in a different location via telephone line. National computer networks provide the user with an opportunity to access a wide variety of programs in institutional research or in management that are located in the computing facilities of other institutions (Johnson and others, 1980). Using computer networks permits the use of programs at reduced costs through shared resources (Sampson, 1982). If networking is a desired characteristic for your system, this capability should also be considered in your equipment selection.

Hardware Support. The question of the amount and availability of support for maintaining your hardware equipment after purchase is extremely important. Questions pertaining to hardware support include brand choice, choice of vendor, locality and access to the vendor, availability of service contracts, and the initial equipment warranty. In the case of the vendor, questions to consider include the previous experience of the vendor in the computer business, the experience of the vendor in the particular needs of an educational institution, and the services available directly through the vendor or dealer. Questions should be asked concerning the length of time needed for equipment repair, as delays can be costly and extremely frustrating. Selecting a local vendor or dealer will eliminate the delays in service caused by distance.

The original equipment warranty should provide for repairs during the break-in period, but another consideration is the purchase of a service or maintenance contract after warranty expiration. A variety of service contracts may be offered by the dealer. These include contracts that provide full on-site service in the case of a breakdown, contracts that require the user to take the equipment in for the necessary service, and contracts that provide for coverage of a portion of the repair costs. When considering the purchase of a service contract, talk to other users of equipment of the same brand name and vendor, if possible, to discuss their experience with the frequency and costs involved in repairs. In the case of equipment with high reliability levels and manufacturer and dealer reputation, purchasing a service contract may prove to be an unneeded expense. You must decide at that point how much risk you are willing to accept.

Training and Documentation. Documentation refers to the manuals, instructions, specifications, and other written training materials. It is important to review the amount and type of documentation that is available for the equipment and software packages you may be considering and also to determine whether the materials are provided with the purchase of the system or whether there is an additional cost.

Equally important is the extent of training available for the use of the computer hardware and for the software packages you may be considering. You should determine whether the necessary training is provided as part of the purchase price or whether extensive additional costs will be involved in obtaining staff training. Also, will training be available on site or at the dealer's or manufacturer's location? What amount of training time is needed actually to implement the programs you are considering?

Training also may be available through your campus's computer center, particularly if you are implementing a system in cooperation with the center or if you have selected software that will run on the center's existing equipment. If you have chosen this alternative, find out in advance what kind of training will be provided and the cost.

Prices. Prices for microcomputers suitable for student development applications vary widely. On our campus an investigation of recent purchases indicates an average range of from approximately $5,000 to $20,000 for microcomputing equipment (not including software development or software packages). Prices generally depend on the brand of equipment and size of the equipment in terms of memory, storage capacity, and number of monitors desired. When comparing prices among dealers and manufacturers, also investigate what is included in the basic purchase price. For example, does the price quoted include all the cables and peripheral equipment required to run the software system desired? Also, what will be the cost for equipment and parts needed for the future expansion of the system — for example, for the purchase of a color or color graphics monitor, the addition of disc drives to increase storage capabilities, and so on?

In addition to price comparisons, you should investigate the possibility of alternative financing options. These include fixed-term leases, lease plans with the future option to purchase, and rental agreements. Leasing equipment may prove to be more costly in the long run, but it also gives you the option of testing the equipment over a period of time long enough to determine its effectiveness for your needs and for running the software you require.

Summary

Key to the selection of computer hardware and software for student development applications is the thorough and systematic analysis of user needs and expectations. Until this task has been completed by the actual users of the system, selection of software and hardware cannot be undertaken. Once the users have identified their needs and established their priorities, the investigation of specific software and hardware packages can begin. With the existing and rapidly growing number of software and hardware options available for use or purchase, this task can be time consuming and complex. Spending the time in comparing software and hardware characteristics to the needs you hope to meet should pay off in your making the best choice possible.

References

Grosswirth, M. "Big Deal for Small Business." *Personal Computing,* August 1983, p. 139.

Hurley, D. E. "A User-Based Systems Analysis Technique." *College and University,* 1981, *56* (2), 167–177.

Johnson, J., Knezek, G., Leighton, J., Lennox, C., McGuigan, J., Shoemaker, C., and Smallen, D. "The EDUNET Experience: Users' Views at Cheminede, Cornell, Delaware, Hamilton, and Mills." *EDUCOM,* 1980, *15* (2), 8–13.

Bruce Riesenberg is acting director of the Career Planning and Placement Center at the University of California–Irvine. He currently serves as a consultant and trainer for LEARN, a project funded by the W. K. Kellogg Foundation.

Achieving success with computer applications has more to do with effective management strategies than with technological sophistication.

Effectively Managing Computer Resources

James P. Sampson, Jr.

Computer applications in student development can be either a blessing or a curse. Used effectively, computer technology can improve services by providing rapid access to vast amounts of information. Used ineffectively, this resource can create confusion and frustration for both students and staff members. When problems occur with computer applications, people have a tendency to look to improvements in hardware and software for solutions. Many of the problems associated with computer technology in student development, however, have little to do with hardware and software. What is needed is not improved technology but, rather, improved strategies for using existing computer resources.

This chapter discusses the evolution of computer applications in student development and the impact of recent technological advances on practitioners in this field. Potential problems associated with computer applications are presented with a suggested approach for effective computer resource management.

Evolution of Computer Applications

Reviewing the evolution of computer use in student development can help you to understand the dynamics involved in managing

C. S. Johnson, K. R. Pyle (Eds.). *Enhancing Student Development with Computers.*
New Directions for Student Services, no. 26. San Francisco: Jossey-Bass, June 1984.

these resources. The initial application of computers to this field occurred at large institutions in the areas of budgeting, student records, registration, and financial aid. To be cost-effective, these applications needed to involve large data bases requiring frequent processing. Computer hardware at this point was usually limited to large mainframe computers oriented toward batch processing of punched cards. Later, the development of more efficient mainframe systems allowed the use of interactive batch processing from remote terminals located around the campus.

These large mainframe computer systems tended to be complicated and difficult to use. Also, because little computer software was generally available in the student development field, each campus needed to develop its own applications. As a result, numerous computer programmers and systems analysts were needed to develop, operate, and maintain the necessary software. For the first time, a significant portion of the tasks associated with designing and operating student services were being completed by individuals outside of the student development profession.

The general reaction to this situation was varied. Some student development staff members adapted rapidly by participating actively in the design and operation of new systems. These staff members became adept at understanding computer jargon, at using complicated mainframe operating procedures, and at working effectively with programmers and analysts who tended to have backgrounds different from student development educators. Other staff members had difficulty in adapting to the changes created in their work environment by the computer. They found the terminology and the operational procedures related to computer use to be confusing and frustrating. They also found it difficult to relate effectively to computer specialists, who tended to have a more quantitative perspective on problem solving.

The problems that some student development staff members have experienced with computer applications have encouraged the belief that the computer dictates how a task will be completed, rather than a staff member deciding on an outcome and then using the computer as a tool to achieve that objective. The assumption that student development staff members have little ability to control the impact of computers has resulted in lower staff morale and, ultimately, less effective student services.

Changing Perspectives

These assumptions are slowly changing, partly through advancements in computer hardware and software but primarily as a result of the willingness of student development staff members to assume more responsibility in designing and operating computer applications. One important factor that has influenced this trend is the growing general acceptance of computer technology in the home. Small personal computers are being sold in a variety of retail establishments to provide educational instruction, entertainment, and home financial management. It is easier to accept technological innovation in the office when that same technology is available at the local elementary school, the bank, and the house next door.

Innovations in computer hardware are also having an impact on the assumption of new roles by staff members. The availability of microcomputers has greatly altered the nature of computing on the college campus. Microcomputers are less expensive, easier to maintain, and easier to operate. As a result, computing on campus is becoming more decentralized. It is now cost effective for many smaller student development operations to utilize computer technology. Only when large data processing tasks are required is it necessary to use the more powerful mainframe computer. The average data processing needs of most student development operations can be adequately handled by a microcomputer.

Recent developments in microcomputer software is another factor influencing staff members to assume a greater role in the design and operation of computer applications. Much of the software available for the microcomputer is intended for use by persons with little computer expertise. Applications, such as data base management, electronic spread sheet systems (for budget analysis), and word processing can be designed and implemented by student development staff members themselves. Because fewer applications today require the increased data processing power of the mainframe computer, campus computer personnel are less directly involved in the provision of student services.

The above trends suggest that student development staff members who in the past were reluctant to assume an active role in using computer technology will now be more inclined to take control over the design and operation of computer applications in their respective areas. The willingness of staff members to assume responsibility for managing computer resources is the most important factor in ensuring that this technology is more of an asset than a liability.

Potential Problems Associated with Computer Applications

The effectiveness of computer applications in student development is at least partially dependent on the ability of staff members to anticipate and prevent potential problems. It is unrealistic to assume that all the potential difficulties associated with computer technology can be eliminated. It is possible, however, to reduce the chances of repeating our previous mistakes. A necessary first step involves identifying problems that have in the past limited the positive impact of computer technology. Such potential problems include: (1) inadequate planning, (2) incompatible hardware and software, (3) inappropriate use of computer center staff, (4) legal and ethical issues, and (5) inadequate implementation.

Inadequate Planning. Poor performance of computer applications is often the result of inadequate planning. Hurley (1981) contends that the failure of system designers to assess user needs adequately has been a major reason that computer applications have not performed as expected. In some cases, too much emphasis has been placed on writing computer programs, and too little emphasis has been placed on determining how a computer application will be integrated into other computerized and noncomputerized functions. For example, a residence hall system might accurately assign rooms according to preference for campus location but fail to permit physically disabled students to request rooms with appropriate access characteristics; in such a case, a major design requirement was overlooked during the planning of the system.

Incompatible Hardware and Software. Over the past five years, the number of options for purchase of computer hardware and software has increased dramatically, particularly in relation to microcomputers. As hardware and software options increase, the chances of purchasing incompatible equipment and programs also increase. For example, differences in operating systems, file structures, and communications protocols can make it difficult, if not impossible, to interconnect various types of micro-, mini-, and mainframe computers without great expense.

A related problem exists with computer software. If, for example, the housing office and the registrar purchase microcomputers with incompatible data base management software, it is quite likely that data from one system cannot be used by the other system. As a result, the two offices must collect and maintain duplicate information, which reduces the cost-effectiveness of the computer application. Similar problems can occur with word processing and electronic spread sheet software.

Inappropriate Use of Computer Center Staff. Some institutions have had a tendency to overutilize or underutilize computer center staff members. For example, the student affairs office may depend on computer center staff to carry out the design and operation of various applications with minimal input from student development personnel. But the heavy work load of computer personnel can often cause delays in providing services, leaving computer staff feeling frustrated and out of control.

On the other end of the continuum, the student affairs office may involve computer staff only marginally in the design and operation process. This results in wasted time and resources if the office must ask computer staff to correct design problems that could have been prevented if a cooperative development process had been utilized. Failure to use computer staff in an appropriate consultative role, by either overdependence or underdependence on their expertise, makes the process of developing computer applications much less efficient.

Legal and Ethical Issues. The misuse of computers in student development has created a variety of legal and ethical dilemmas. One legal issue involves the security of data maintained on the computer. A small number of students each year gains access to restricted computer files by obtaining confidential passwords illegally. Most incidents involve altering academic records, destruction of files, or theft of computer time. Powers (1980) cautions that a breach of security is a possibility at any computer installation. Clearly, there is a need to implement the best available security procedures as well as to develop appropriate student judicial procedures for this situation.

Another legal issue involves copyright protection of computer software. Some institutions have attempted to protect the investment of time and financial resources associated with software development by copyrighting computer programs. It is often difficult, however, to determine copyright ownership as well as to identify instances where violations have occurred (Lautsch, 1979). Examples might include software that is written in cooperation with another organization or programs that include previously copyrighted lines of code.

In addition, the use of computers in student development raises a variety of ethical questions; these issues are discussed in Chapter Six.

Inadequate Implementation. The potential effectiveness of computer applications has been limited in some cases because of poor implementation practices. For example, staff members have often been unsupportive of new computer applications in the mental health field when there has been a lack of: (1) organizational readiness for change, (2) a planned change strategy, and (3) a method of dealing with staff resistance (Byrnes & Johnson, 1981). Other causes of staff resistance include insufficient staff participation in decision making (Kiresuk and others, 1980) and a fear of being replaced by the computer (Joiner and others, 1980; Super, 1973). It is interesting to note that these problems have more to do with human relations than with technology.

Computer Resource Management

Computer resource management can contribute to overall effectiveness of student services by providing an organized method for dealing with potential problems and a clear delineation of staff responsibilities. This approach assumes that student development staff members are willing to take an active role in the design and operation of computer applications. The following model for computer resource management (Sampson, 1982) suggests general guidelines for staff responsibilities. Specific assignment of responsibilities will depend on the size and organization of the student development staff. Unless large data processing operations are involved, the individual should be able to complete the tasks described here as part of his or her regular activities.

Project Leader. The project leader has direct responsibility for the design and operation of a computer application — for example, a placement center staff member who has responsibility for a computer-assisted interview scheduling system. Three major tasks exist for this staff member. First, the project leader oversees the development or revision of original software. This includes:

- Identifying staff members who will complete software development
- Articulating the needs identified in the planning process to the staff members who will design the software
- Coordinating the efforts of the programmers so that, as much as possible, all software elements are completed on schedule and at about the same time
- Conducting regular evaluations during the software development phase to determine if identified needs are being met
- Conducting tests of the completed software to ensure that performance expectations are achieved
- Ensuring that adequate documentation has been written so that programmers can revise the software without wasting time trying to figure out how the program functions
- Ensuring that backup copies of the software and of any data files are available if the original programs and files are destroyed by staff error or hardware failure
- Integrating any new operational procedures into staff training materials
- Supervising operation of the computer application within the institution
- Conducting regular evaluations of software and hardware performance.

Second, the project leader is responsible for ensuring that all computer hardware is maintained adequately. And third, the project leader is responsible for staying aware of new computer applications that relate to his or her specific field.

Chief Student Affairs Officer. Computer resource management tasks that affect the total student development program or the institution in general become the responsibility of the chief student affairs officer (CSAD). Large institutions may delegate many of the following tasks to directors or coordinators of specific functions (housing, for example). In any case, maximum success in computer resource management is only achieved when the activities of the CSAD or designate are closely coordinated with the efforts of project leaders.

Four specific computer resource management responsibilities exist for the CSAD. The first responsibility involves planning for future computer applications. This process begins with an analysis of existing and future needs as well as an examination of how new applications would relate to existing services. Hurley (1981) presents a services/requirements analysis approach that "provides a user-directed vehicle for establishing and defining information needs within the various organizational units" (p. 174). Erwin and Tollefson (1982) describe a data base management system that integrates a new computer application with existing services. After completing a needs analysis and exploring the relationships between old and new systems, the CSAD can go into more detailed planning for software development. The project leader is heavily involved in this process.

The second responsibility of the CSAD or designate involves implementation of computer applications. This includes initiating staff participation in decision making and developing a planned change strategy. Ensuring that effective staff development programs are designed and conducted is another important aspect of implementation. Specific steps involved in implementing computer applications are provided by C. Johnson (1980), J. Johnson (1980), Sampson (1984), Schoech and others (1981), and Taylor (1981).

The third responsibility of the CSAD involves regular evaluation of the effectiveness of computer applications. Factors such as the cost of hardware, software, and staff time need to be evaluated in light of the impact of computer applications on the provision of services. The rapid rate of change in computer technology, especially the rapid advances in hardware, can dramatically alter the cost effectiveness of a specific application; for example, many institutions experienced greatly improved cost effectiveness when they transferred some applications from large mainframe systems to microcomputers.

The fourth responsibility of the CSAD involves ensuring that computer applications are used in a legally and ethically appropriate manner. Specific issues that need attention include confidentiality of student records, copyright registration, and the need for staff intervention with students who use various computer applications.

Computer Resource Coordinator. The computer resource coordinator (CRC) is responsible for completing tasks that require specialized expertise in managing the use of computer hardware and software. The perspective of the CRC encompasses the entire student development field, while the perspective of the project leader is generally limited to a specific service area. The CRC is used most effectively in a consulting role with the CSAD and the project leaders.

The first responsibility of the CRC involves coordinating the purchasing of computer hardware and software. By examining the characteristics of various equipment and program options prior to purchase, the CRC reduces the chances of compatability problems.

The second responsibility of the CRC involves providing project leaders with information on recent hardware and software innovations. This information can be obtained from vendors, computer networks, and personal contacts with computer center personnel.

The third responsibility of the CRC involves serving as a liaison with the campus computer center. In this way, the CRC can inform project leaders of new campus computer resources as well as of changes in operating procedures that affect their specific applications. The computer center staff can receive feedback on computer performance as well as information on future data processing needs. The CRC also can facilitate appropriate use of computer center staff members by guarding against overdependence or underdependence on their expertise.

Summary

Computer applications in student development clearly have the potential to enhance student services if we can learn from our past experiences and take full advantage of the recent advances in computer hardware and software. In addition to improving existing functions, the computer can deliver a wide range of previously unavailable services. For example, students can have rapid and direct access to information resources that support personal, social, educational, and career development. These information resources can be accessed from a variety of locations, such as a campus residence hall, a local apartment, or the home of a prospective student a thousand miles away.

The availability of computer applications that meet student

needs is both a design and a management issue. The key to effective management of computer resources lies in the willingness of student development staff members actively to participate in directing the use of this technology.

References

Byrnes, E., and Johnson, J. H. "Change Technology and the Implementation of Automation in Mental Health Care Settings." *Behavior Research Methods and Instrumentation,* 1981, *13,* 573–580.

Erwin, T. D., and Tollefson, A. L. "A Data Base Management Model for Student Development." *Journal of College Student Personnel,* 1982, *23,* 70–76.

Hurley, D. E. "A User-Based Systems Analysis Technique." *College and University,* 1981, *56* (2), 167–177.

Johnson, C. S. "Five-Stage Model of Implementation of Computer-Assisted Guidance." Unpublished manuscript, Michigan State University, 1980.

Johnson, J. H. "A Practical Guide to Installing a Computer System in a Mental Health Setting." In J. B. Sidowski, J. H. Johnson, and T. A. Williams (Eds.), *Technology in Mental Health Care Delivery Systems.* Norwood, N.J.: Ablex, 1980.

Joiner, L. M., Miller, S. R., and Silverstein, B. J. "Potential and Limits of Computers in Schools." *Educational Leadership,* 1980, *37,* 498–501.

Kiresuk, T. J., Davis, H. R., and Lund, S. H. "Knowledge Utilization and Planned Change in the Mental Health Services." In J. B. Sidowski, J. H. Johnson, and T. A. Williams (Eds.), *Technology in Mental Health Care Delivery Systems.* Norwood, N.J.: Ablex, 1980.

Lautsch, J. C. "Computers and the University Computer: An Overview of Computer Law on Campus." *Journal of College and University Law,* 1979, *5,* 217–280.

Powers, D. E. "How Safe Is Your Computer?" *Creative Computing,* 1980, *6,* 32, 34–35.

Sampson, J. P., Jr. "Effective Computer Resource Management: Keeping the Tail from Wagging the Dog." *NASPA Journal,* 1982, *19* (3), 38–46.

Sampson, J. P., Jr. "The Use of Computers." In H. D. Burck and R. C. Reardon (Eds.), *Career Development Interventions.* Springfield, Ill.: Thomas, 1984.

Schoech, D. J., Schkade, L. L., and Mayers, R. S. "Strategies for Information System Development." *Administration and Social Work,* 1981, *5* (3/4), 11–26.

Super, D. E. "Computers in Support of Vocational Development and Counseling." In H. Borow (Ed.), *Career Guidance for a New Age.* Boston: Houghton Mifflin, 1973.

Taylor, J. B. *Using Microcomputers in Social Agencies.* Beverly Hills, Calif.: Sage, 1981.

*James P. Sampson, Jr., is an assistant professor in the
Department of Human Services and Studies at Florida State
University in Tallahassee, Florida.*

Computers have been in use for almost two decades in the area of computer-assisted career guidance. The historical development of this direct student access application has implications for other uses of computer technology.

Computer-Assisted Guidance: An Example of Direct Student Access

Cynthia S. Johnson

Computer-assisted guidance systems were the first example of a computer application for direct student use in student affairs. Computers were used for three decades for instruction, management, and research in higher education (Joiner and others, 1980), but it was not until the mid 1960s that computers became a tool to assist student affairs in career guidance. Now, millions of dollars have been spent on the development of career-related software packages, and extensive research and field testing have been conducted in this area for two decades.

This chapter describes the historical development of computer-assisted career guidance and information systems, reviews the current state of the art, and takes a look at some exciting trends for the future.

Historical Development

The "Fourth Revolution" in higher education, as predicted by Sir Eric Ashby in 1967 (Carnegie Commission, 1972), has arrived.

Portions of this article were published in the *International Journal for the Advancement of Counseling,* 1983, *6,* 134–141. "Shaping Counselor Education Programs," G. Walz and L. Benjamin, ERIC/CAPS, 1983.

C. S. Johnson, K. R. Pyle (Eds.). *Enhancing Student Development with Computers.*
New Directions for Student Services, no. 26. San Francisco: Jossey-Bass, June 1984.

45

enhance the growth, decision-making skills, and problem-solving abilities of individuals" (283–287). Research evidence cited by Harris-Bowlsbey (1974), Pyle and Stripling (1976), Katz (1980), and Wagman and Kerber (1980) supported this conclusion.

At the same time, computer costs steadily decreased, making the technology more accessible. And funding for costly software and sophisticated development and testing was made available by organizations such as International Business Machines (IBM), the Carnegie Corporation of New York, and the Department of Labor.

Both hardware and software have progressed significantly since the early systems of guidance were developed. But attitudinal resistance on the part of professionals, financial difficulties, and lack of knowledge and training needed to integrate these tools into a total program continue to present barriers to the successful implementation of computers in the career guidance professional's work.

Current State of the Art

While all the early problems have not been resolved, much progress has been made in the past two decades. Currently there are more than thirty-five computer-based guidance systems operating at more than 7,000 sites (see Figure 1). These systems fall into two general categories: information retrieval, and interactive guidance and information. They are found in high schools, colleges, public libraries, and other locations. The infusion of federal dollars for labor market data and vocational education, with technological breakthroughs, increased sophistication on the part of the professional, and increased demand for services by a wide range of clients have all contributed to the expansion the use of computers in career guidance.

The availability of low-cost, desktop microcomputers is also making a significant difference in the number of users. SIGI, for example, doubled its sales in 1983 with the new microcomputer version. Most current systems are available on microcomputers.

Current information retrieval systems include the previously mentioned Career Information System (CIS) and the Guidance Information System (GIS), which provides current and accurate occupational information as well as useful data about undergraduate and graduate programs and professional schools. GIS does not have a guidance component, leaving that function to the counselor.

Computerized Heuristic Occupation Information and Career Exploration System (CHOICES), originally developed for use in Canada, is now used in several states in the United States. Other major

Figure 1. Descriptions of Current Systems

Systems	Representative	Settings Used	Assessing Strategy(s)	Information Components
CIS (Career Information System)	1969 (OIAS) Dr. Bruce McKinlay 247 Hendricks Hall University of Oregon Eugene, OR 97403	Secondary schools; voc., tech., and comm. col.; four-year colleges; corrections; CETA; voc. rehab.; and others	Structured search: quest twenty-one user perferences or any combination.	Occupation files: local occupations (numbers vary between states); preparation; bibliography. Educ. file: training programs, colleges and tech./voc. schools (local). Other files: high school visits, summer jobs, and employers.
CHOICES (Computerized Heuristic Occupation Information Career Exploration System)	Robert J. Alexander CSG Corporation 1101 Connecticut Washington, DC 20036	Employment offices; some high schools, community colleges, and universities	Structured search: explore 150 user-selected variables. Direct access: to any file any time; specific information on chosen occ. compare requirements for two or three occ.'s; related occ.'s to user-selected occupation. Off line: travel guide; self-directed search; GATB & Canada interest test	Occ. File: 1,100 primary occ's (occ's localized into twelve provincial data files). Institutional file: all public postsecondary institutions in Canada; 47,500 unique training programs.

Figure 1. Descriptions of Current Systems (*continued*)

Systems	Representative	Settings Used	Assessing Strategy(s)	Information Components
COIN (Coordinated Occupational Information Network)	1978 Dr. Rodney Durgan COIN, Inc. 1230 West Wooster Bowling Green, Ohio 43402	Secondary schools; CETA; voc. rehab.; and others	Structured search: user-created occupational profile; college search. Direct access: to any file any time; self-directed search.	Occ. file: 280 occ.'s (national data); capability of inserting local wage and outlook data. Educ. files: college majors; two- and four-year colleges; apprenticeship. Other files: military school subjects.
CVIS (Computerized Vocational Information System)	1967 Carol M. Rabush CVIS Distribution Center Western Maryland College Westminster, MD 21157	Secondary schools, two- and four-year colleges	Structured search: compares student preferences to Holland's classifications; college search. Direct access: to any file any time.	Occ. file: 430 occ.'s (national data). Educ. files: 1600 institutions in college search file. Others: military script.
DISCOVER	1976 Se. JoAnn Harris-Bowlsbey DISCOVER 230 Schilling Circle Hunt Valley, MD 21031	Secondary schools, two- and four-year colleges values, interests, and	Guidance process: learning modules on values, interests, and competencies, decision making, career planning, grouping occ.'s and job search. Direct access: getting information about occupations.	Occ. file 450 + occ.'s (national data). Educ. file: 1,000 two-year colleges; 1,100 tech. schools; 600 graduate schools; 450 military training programs; financial aid; apprenticeships.

GIS III (Guidance Information System)	1971 Linda Kowlarz Time Share 630 Oakwood Avenue West Hartford, Connecticut 06110	Secondary schools, Voc./tech. schools, CETA; corrections, two- four-year colleges, voc. rehab., and others	Structured search: user-selected variables. Direct access: not reported.	Occ. file: 850 occ.'s (national data); several state files. Educ. files: 1600 + 4-year colleges; 1400 two-year colleges; graduate schools. Other files: job bank, armed services, scholarships, and career resources.
SIGI (System of Interactive Guidance and Information)	1972 Dr. Martin Katz Educational Testing Service Princeton, NJ 08591	Two- four-year colleges, some higher schools, manpower offices, private counseling	Guidance process: values clarification (ten occ. values examined); relates values to occ.'s; compares occ.'s on various topics; matches values, occ.'s, and predictions; prediction or college programs (must be localized); relates training to occupations (must be localized).	Educational files: national data.

Figure 2. Features of Current Systems

Systems	Job Search	Varied Media	Other Languages	Other Features
CIS	Refers user to employment services	Needle-sort cards (Quest; Printed occ.'s and educational information and microfiche)	no	Extensive information development at state level; implemented in wide-range settings as a statewide information system (eight states)
CHOICES	Compatible with Canada's METRO Order processing system (job bank)	Print occ.'s	French (Spanish and German to be added)	Very flexible, accessing occ.'s
COIN	South Carolina job bank to be added	Microfiche	no	
CVIS	Some CVIS versions tied to local job banks	no	no	Very flexible, accessing occ.'s or colleges
DISCOVER	Local jobs module leads to local information on job employment services, job bank, job search information, resume and interview information	no	no	Entry module for new users; on line evaluation component; extensive assistance with values, decision making, and career planning.
GIS III	no	microfiche	no	Implemented in wide range of settings and in several states (GIS-III version).
SIGI	no	no	no	Extensive assistance with understanding values.

systems currently in operation include the Coordinated Occupational Information Network (COIN); Educational and Career Exploration System (ECES); and System Exploration and Research for Career Help (SEARCH).

Major systems currently in use that provide on line and interactive guidance, in addition to occupational information, include DISCOVER I and II, developed by Harris-Bowlsbey, and Katz's SIGI. DISCOVER offers interest inventories, aptitude tests, value ratings, and other appraisal techniques on line. For example, the user is able to take the Self-Directed Search, the Strong-Campbell Inventory, or the Kuder test on the computer and receive their scores on the screen. Twenty questions about current salaries, educational requirements, and so on may be asked about various occupations. Colleges, universities, and technical school that provide training for careers or occupations may be located. A job bank is also available. In DISCOVER, test scores are matched with occupations and jobs that meet the specific profile of the user. DISCOVER, now part of American College Testing (ACT), has a variety of versions for different kinds of computers and for different populations (such as business people or high school students).

The Future

The near future will bring new, more sophisticated technology to bear on societal problems of the older adult in some state of career transition. It has been estimated (Aslanian, 1981) that there are some forty million adults in America in some stage of life transition. Many of them seek new career choices because of underemployment, unemployment, divorce, mid-life crises, or the current economy, to name a few reasons.

With the generous support of the W. K. Kellogg Foundation under a grant from the Council for the Advancement of Experiential Learning (CAEL) called Project LEARN, researchers are developing two adult computer-assisted guidance systems: ETS is developing an adult version of SIGI for the microcomputer; Harris-Bowlsbey and ACT are developing an adult version of DISCOVER. Both these interactive adult career guidance systems will use the latest in theoretical and technological advances. They will be supported with other software on adult learning styles, adult transitions, and developmental stage assessment. These systems will enable adult learners to make new career decisions, discover their own learning styles, assess previous life experiences for academic credit, select a college setting for further training, and even find a job.

DISCOVER and the adult SIGI working together in sites throughout the country should assist the counselor in the delivery of high-quality, low-cost, sophisticated help for the increasing number of adult learners with diverse needs.

It is certain that the next few years will bring major changes technologically in the way in which counselors are able to do business. Videodiscs, computer graphics, and voice computers are already available. At Florida State University, for example, a voice-activated computer-assisted guidance system is in operation on an experimental basis. Voice commands for disabled students can activate a computer, and the computer will talk back. Additional adaptations have been made on that campus for the partially sighted, the deaf, and the quadraplegic.

DISCOVER II will have videodiscs available in 1984 on hundreds of occupations. The client will be able to ask questions about an occupational field and look at a colored video display of that occupation that includes a look at the actual work environment. DISCOVER III is now available to address the needs of business and industry.

More vendors will be attempting to enter the market with competing and, in some cases, conflicting software packages, and decisions about which computer to purchase and what system to use will become more complex.

Role of the Professional. Professionals will need to address the issue (covered in Chapter Two) of how to select hardware and software. What are the theoretic foundations of various software programs? Does an information retrieval system or a guidance system best meet the needs of specific client populations? Many systems present theoretical foundations that are diametrically opposed. Which philosophical base most closely approximates that of the counselor—that is, how does the system compare and contrast with the counseling theory of the professional? Of the center or work environment? Analysis of content by professionals is critical, yet decisions sometimes are being made without addressing these concerns.

Hardware selection is a second problem. With the rapid development and increasing availability of new, low-cost computers, questions of compatibility, versatility, and obsolescence need to be considered. Chapter Two has addressed these concerns.

A lack of personnel training to utilize the computer effectively as an intervention in counseling currently exists. None of the major computer programs are meant to stand alone. They require a trained professional to assist the client through the decision-making process and to intervene when necessary. Few counselor training programs currently provide training in computer competency and counseling.

And, finally, as stated by Sampson in Chapter Three, managers need to be trained in how to implement and manage computers effectively. Obtaining appropriate agency or institutional support and deciding where to house the computer are issues not previously addressed by counseling managers. Many costly errors have been made once a computer system has been purchased through lack of knowledge about the management and implementation of computer technology.

Role of the Profession. The profession as a whole needs to address the ethical issues and standards described by Sampson in Chapter Six. The computer can have a negative impact on the client when unethical procedures are utilized or no standards exist. For example, no code exists that addresses the confidentiality of client records on a computer or the potential abuse of client information when the computer is used as a research tool without client permission. There is a need for appropriately trained counselors to intervene when computer technology raises anxieties. Standards for the content of computer information must also be written. Some programs, for example, contain outdated and erroneous occupational information.

Role of Professional Associations. The following are suggested tasks that professional associations can accomplish in the technological revolution:

- Development of an ethical statement and minimum standards for the use of technology consistent with the American Psychological Association and the American Association of Counseling and Development (formerly the American Personnel and Guidance Association).
- Assistance in promoting computer literacy as part of the training and professional development of counselors. (A certificate program might be considered. In addition, professional associations should urge graduate preparation programs to include computer literacy in the curriculum for future professionals.)
- Provision by one or more of the associations of a clearinghouse for software programs and for research on their effectiveness. (Very few software programs are available to the student development profession. Software development lags far behind that of hardware, and because software development can be costly, professionals should be encouraged to share program development so that everyone does not need to reinvent the wheel.)

- Establishment of a review procedure. (Once a critical mass of software is accumulated, professional associations should establish a formal review procedure and publish it on a regular basis in their professional journals just as they publish book reviews.)
- Assistance from outside agencies. (Federal agencies should be asked to supply funds for initial software development and testing; pressure should be placed on local, state, and federal agencies by the associations.)

Finally, associations should take the lead in assisting professionals not only to catch up to the revolution but also to get ahead of it. Future issues concerning the application of videodiscs, videotext, and teletext are already being addressed by some educational organizations. These matters have serious implications for the counseling profession, and professional associations should provide the necessary leadership.

Summary

Computer technology is new to the student affairs profession, but many gains have occurred in the development of computer software and in counselor sophistication since pioneers like Harris-Bowlsbey began their work in the field in the mid 1960s.

This chapter has reviewed the development of computer-assisted information and guidance software over the past two decades. Professional associations now need to propose an ethical statement and minimum standards of operation. Associations should also provide leadership in sponsoring professional development activities to teach computer literacy, in providing support for computer courses in graduate training programs, and in developing networks, software reviews, and clearinghouses for the exchange of software programs and ideas.

The technology is here. Many important advances have been made in the past two decades. Much work needs to be done on the part of the profession in the next few years to take advantage of this amazing new tool that has been added to the counselor's repertoire.

References

Aslanian, C. B. *Americans in Transition: Life Changes as Reasons for Adult Learning.* New York: College Entrance Examination Board, 1981.

Carnegie Commission on Higher Education. *The Fourth Revolution: Instructional Technology in Higher Education.* New York: McGraw-Hill, 1972.

Cross, K. P. *Accent on Learning: Improving Instruction and Reshaping the Curriculum.* San Francisco: Jossey-Bass, 1976.

Harris-Bowlsbey, J. "The Computer: Guidance Tool of the Future." *Journal of Counseling Psychology,* 1974, *21,* 331–339.

Joiner, L. M., Miller, S. R., and Silverstein, B. J. "Potential and Limits of Computers in Schools." *Educational Leadership,* 1980, *37,* 498–501.

Katz, M. R. "SIGI: An Interactive Aid to Career Decision-Making." *Journal of College Student Personnel,* 1980, *21,* 34–40.

Last, A. "Computer-Assisted Guidance in Britain: Will the Developments Be of Use to Adults?" *Journal of Occupational Psychology,* 1978, *51,* 49–53.

Pyle, K. R., and Stripling, R. O. "The Counselor, the Computer, and Career Development." *Vocational Guidance Quarterly,* 1976, *25,* 71–75.

Sampson, J. P., Jr., and Pyle, K. R. "Ethical Issues Involved with the Use of Computer-Assisted Counseling, Testing, and Guidance Systems." *Personnel and Guidance Journal,* 1983, *61,* 283–287.

Shatkin, L., Katz, M. R., Norris, L., Chapman, W., Weber, A., Wood, S. *Computer-Based Guidance: State of the Art.* Princeton, N.J.: Educational Testing Service, 1981.

Wagman, M., and Kerber, K. W. "PLATO DCS, An Interactive Computer System for Personal Counseling: Further Development and Evaluation." *Journal of Counseling Psychology,* 1980, *27,* 31–34.

Whiteley and Resnikoff, A. *Career Counseling.* Monterey, Calif.: Brooks/Cole, 1978.

Cynthia S. Johnson is an assistant professor and cochairperson of the doctoral program in Counseling and Personnel Services, College of Education, University of Maryland. She is currently director of counselor training in the use of technology for adult learners for Project LEARN.

Although not suited for every application, general purpose
software can be a useful method for learning the capabilities
of microcomputers as well as for improving effectiveness and
efficiency in a particular task.

General Purpose
Applications for
Student Development

L. Russell Watjen

The student affairs worker who has access to a microcomputer and is
eager to acquire a special application on line is apt to be sadly disap-
pointed. Except in areas such as career development, there is little or
no software of commercial grade available. The entrance of microcomputers into the field of student development is so recent that very little
commercial software has been produced for the field. Also, very little is
known about the public domain software (that is, software that is free
for the asking) that does exist.

There is, however, a category of high-quality software, known
as general purpose software, that can fill some of the gap that exists
between our needs and the software now available. General purpose
software is just what the name implies: software designed in such a way
that it can be molded by users to serve a variety of purposes. In many
respects, the capabilities of true general purpose software are limited
only by the imagination of its users.

In contrast to general purpose software is special purpose software, which is designed to serve one function. An application program
designed to maintain an inventory of furniture very likely will not be

C. S. Johnson, K. R. Pyle (Eds.). *Enhancing Student Development with Computers.*
New Directions for Student Services, no. 26. San Francisco: Jossey-Bass, June 1984.

adaptable to keeping track of petty cash expenditures. Some special purpose software is so specific in its use that it cannot be used even for the same purpose by a similar organization without extensive modification.

Between the extremes of general purpose software and special purpose software, there exist many gradations. This chapter is concerned primarily with the general purpose end of this continuum; thus, we will look at programs written to handle tasks common to all businesses. Although this software was not designed specifically for student affairs, student development educators may find it very useful and cost-effective.

Some Caveats

Before we discuss some of the more readily available kinds of general purpose programs, some words of caution are in order:

1. When choosing an application that requires large amounts of data entry, be careful to choose a program and hardware that have the capacity to handle both present and future requirements. Many a user has laboriously loaded large amounts of data into a program, only to discover later that the program's capacity has been exceeded. Not only can this mean having to purchase new software but it may also mean having to re-enter the data by keyboard into the new program if the old and the new programs are incompatible.

2. A similar problem arises when the applications contemplated involve manipulation of the same data by more than one program. In this case, be careful to select programs with compatible file structures. A relatively recent development that addresses this problem is the *integrated software package;* it consists essentially of two or more different subprograms integrated into one software program that can manipulate the same files.

3. Do not computerize data that is best left alone. Not everything that can be done on computers should be done on computers. Some things actually take more time when run on computers than when done manually. It is, for example, possible to computerize a daily schedule and, in fact, some people find this a convenient, time-saving device. Many others, however, find they spend more time loading information into the computer system than they would keeping a standard calendar book. There is no easy way to identify such applications in advance, but, as you gain experience, they can be more easily anticipated. The old guideline of "if it isn't broken, don't fix it" usually holds. If the process works well now, if it does not take an inordinate amount

of time or staff, and, if there does not appear to be any particular advantage to computerizing it, the chances are that it would be better to leave it alone. The computer is a powerful tool, but, like all tools, it will perform only as well as its operator permits.

4. Never assume a program will perform a function unless promotional material or manuals say that it will. If the software company does not promote a particular feature, the software probably lacks that function. Even when claims are made that the software includes a particular feature, caution is well advised. The reader who is interested in making comparisons of various work sheet programs, for example, should obtain a recent software directory dealing with software that runs on his or her present or prospective equipment and compare the capabilities of available software packages of the type needed.

Categories of General Purpose Software

The categories of general purpose software covered in this chapter are: electronic work sheet, data base, word processing, graphics, and communications software. Discussion of this software will be of a general nature with little reference to particular software packages unless appropriate due to the software's historical significance. Discussion will proceed from a description of the nature of the software in question to a description of its capabilities and of how it can be used in student development. Finally, a list of factors is provided that are of particular importance in regard to selecting software.

Electronic Work Sheet

No discussion of general purpose software would be complete without discussion of the granddaddy of all general purpose software packages — the electronic work sheet. The program Visicalc (produced by Personal Software, Incorporated) is largely credited with the rapid growth in popularity of the personal computer. This program was so powerful for its time that people are said to have purchased the software package and whatever machine it ran on. Today many microcomputer users continue to be introduced to the capabilities of microcomputers through electronic work sheet programs.

Work Sheet Capabilities. An electronic work sheet is the computerization of the familiar accounting work sheet in a form that is far more flexible than the original. An accounting work sheet is a large grid of rows and columns into which figures are normally entered. At each position on the electronic work sheet, the user can enter labels, numbers, or a formula to be calculated on the basis of values occurring on the work sheet. The result of the computation is recorded in place of the formula. Herein lies one of the strengths of the electronic work sheet: If one of the values on which the formula's results are calculated is changed, the result is automatically recalculated. You can correct errors and omissions instantaneously and without extended recomputation. Erasures and recalculations are handled electronically with speed and accuracy. An electronic work sheet program can be used to replace nearly any function currently handled by means of a calculator, pencil, and sheet of paper.

This description contains important clues to limitations of work sheet programs. Although some organizations handle all of their accounting by means of paper, pencil, and calculator, most organizations with accounting processes of any size use specialized accounting procedures to handle their books. This is true in regard to electronic work sheet programs also. Although some organizations are small enough to get by with only a work sheet program to handle their accounting needs, most of any size opt for special purpose accounting programs that are better suited to more complex accounting requirements.

Some of the newer work sheet programs have become quite complex and have been integrated with other general purpose software. The remainder of this discussion deals with the basic capabilities of work sheet programs.

With a work sheet program, the computer monitor becomes a window that looks out onto a portion of the much larger work sheet. This window can be moved around the work sheet so that the user can view any part of it. The monitor can even be used split-screen for comparing one part of the work sheet with another. Simple arithmetic and logical operations can be performed on the values appearing in fields on the work sheet. Some work sheet programs permit sorting fields in alphabetical or numerical order, merging work sheets, and other desirable options.

Various formatting commands available with work sheet programs permit the user to design screens suited to many different purposes. Insertions and deletions are simple, and, once the general layout for a work sheet is completed, it can be saved on a disc, reproduced, and used repeatedly for the same as well as for other purposes. Electronic work sheets can also be printed out in whole or in part in order to provide hard copy. At least one book is available that gives the commands necessary to produce Visicalc work sheets suited to many different purposes (Castlewitz and others, 1982).

The ability to recalculate outcomes instantaneously also lends the work sheet to use in decision making. You might, for example, use it to look at the total cost of various combinations of equipment purchases before a final decision is made. This form of decision making has been referred to as the "what if" model. The user repeatedly asks, "What if I choose this alternative instead of another?" Appropriate values are substituted and answers calculated instantaneously.

Applications in Student Development. Offices that deal with budgets, student organization accounts, grants, and other processes involving modest columns of figures are likely to find work sheet programs useful. Other areas of application found in student development include the comparison of data, such as those related to various applicants for a position. If criteria can be quantified and weighted, indices can be calculated automatically and factors compared.

A related but less obvious application of work sheet programs involves manipulation of nonquantifiable data in an application that resembles word processing. Taking advantage of the rows and columns appearing in work sheets and using the labeling (or typing) function, you can list candidates for a position down one side of a work sheet, while criteria and desirable traits are listed across the top of the work sheet. By filling in the rows and columns with information relating to candidates, you can see at a glance how various individuals compare. Using the move and insert capabilities found in work sheet programs, you can add columns for additional characteristics and make direct comparisons of finalists.

Selection Factors. When selecting an electronic work sheet program, you should consider the following useful characteristics:

- Will the program interface with other software packages?
- Are column widths variable?
- What is the program's capacity or its size limitations?
- What special functions are available?
- Are report (output) formats flexible?

Electronic File Cabinet or Data Base

The term data base is familiar to most persons working in institutions of higher education. Data bases are as common in the lives of twentieth century educators as are the telephone and automobile. Most people, however, are not aware of how dependent we are on these devices. The most readily identifiable data base is the telephone book. Other well-known data bases are the dictionary, the department store catalogue, and the library card catalogue. These applications share one characteristic in common that qualifies them as data base — that is, information used in a wide variety of applications is organized centrally and in such a manner as to make it easy to locate a single piece of information quickly and easily.

Victor Baldridge (1983) in an address to the American College Personnel Association's convention in Houston, Texas, noted that, of all society's institutions, none is more heavily involved in the information business than higher education. Institutions of higher education are inundated with information regarding students, faculty, and class size. Thus, the manually constructed data bases that served us well in the past are rapidly being replaced by computerized data bases because of the great speed and flexibility offered by computerized access.

A data base system is a set of related programs allowing the user to design a file and to enter data into this file. Words or numbers on which searches are to be based are defined as *keys*. Once organized and stored, data can be retrieved, updated, reorganized, and printed out in any of a virtually unlimited number of report formats. Of great importance in the development of a data base is the planning that takes place prior to determining file structure. The information to be collected must be decided in advance.

An institution's student data base, for example, is made up of all student records. Student records are, in turn, made up of a series of fields containing information such as age, sex, major, address, and date of birth. Each record contains similar kinds of information organized around a key number, letter, or word. In the case of a student record, this key might be the student's name or social security number.

Data Base Capabilities. Data base programs perform operations such as creating, sorting, or revising files and generating reports from stored information. In addition, some data base programs permit the use of programming techniques to perform special operations on records within the data base. Many data base programs have the ability to compute percentages, totals, and other functions such as storing information in designated fields and printing results according to prearranged formats. Records can be identified and/or summarized based on such criteria as a range of values (for example, the program can list the names of persons whose salaries fall within a certain range). Specific characteristics, such as sex and geographic location, can also be used as parameters for a search.

Applications to Student Affairs Work. Most data base applications used in student development are probably best left on the larger minicomputer and mainframe systems. This is due to the limited memory capacities of microcomputers and the need for access to the same information by offices in various parts of the campus. Microcomputers can be used, however, as terminals to update a central data base, allowing access to information about a particular item, such as a student's address, and there are a number of data base applications in student development that do lend themselves to microcomputers. Typical of such applications are the preparation of mailing lists, the scheduling of events, and the analysis of some statistics.

Selection Factors. In considering data base software, you should look at the following program characteristics:

- Ability to interface with other programs
- Ability to calculate summary statistics
- Flexible input and output formats
- Ability to sort on key words
- Disc storage requirements and system capacity requirements
- Power of search and select functions
- System security and the ability to protect fields
- Accommodation of a variety of data formats by the system
- Degree of difficulty encountered in revising record formats once they are defined.

Word Processing

Probably the most widely known (and certainly the most widely publicized) general purpose application of microcomputer technology is word processing. Essentially, word processing involves the recording of written information on a cathode ray tube (CRT) and storing it on a magnetic disc prior to final transfer to paper. The advantage of such a system is that information can be corrected, revised, and updated instantaneously without having to retype information that has not changed. Time and productivity losses are significant when manual corrections are necessary, as is the case with a typewriter.

The *electronic typewriter* is the simplest equipment that can be used for word processing. In contrast to *electric* typewriters, which are primarily mechanical devices driven by electricity, an electronic typewriter relies on electronics for its speed and capabilities. Until the last stages of word processing, the written word is recorded and stored electronically either in computer memory or on electronic media such as the floppy disc. In the end, however, most word processors must still resort to an electromechanical printer for output.

Word Processing Capabilities. How often do individuals read a document that has been forwarded only to find embarrassing errors that have gone undetected? How often do people settle for documents that are less than perfect because they cannot justify the time and aggravation involved in retyping the document? An important capability provided by the word processor is the ability to make changes and corrections with a minimum of effort and almost no waste.

Unless you possess the ability to remember the spelling of most words, there is another attractive capability that comes with many word processors: the spelling checker. The word processor can check through dictionaries of 80,000 words or more in a matter of minutes. Most spelling checkers can mark words as misspelled for correction, add words to the dictionary, and create specialized dictionaries suited to particular applications. An equally attractive feature of word processors is the ability to identify typographical errors, thus permitting the less-than-expert typist to purge text of these errors.

In addition to these basic capabilities, most word processors have one or more of the following capabilities: the ability to merge documents; the ability to produce multiple originals; the ability to replace a given word in one or more places in the document with a pre-defined word; and the ability to move entire phrases or blocks of text from one location in the document to another. Some word processing systems permit split-screen operation so that the typist can view two separate parts of the document at the same time. Still other systems permit generation of personalized form letters with the insertion of names from an address list. The list of options possible with word processors seems limited only by the capacity of present machines to contain the programs. With ever-increasing computer storage capacities, the options available will continue to expand.

Applications in Student Development Work. Applications of word processing technology to student development are even more varied than are applications of the typewriter. Personalized form letters, report preparation, publications preparation, and memoranda of all types are but a few of the readily identifiable applications. When used in conjunction with communications equipment, a word processor is capable of preparing files that can be rapidly transmitted, received, and reviewed by the addressee without ever having been committed to paper.

Selection Factors. When selecting word processing software, be sure you ask the following questions:

- Does the document being typed appear accurately on the monitor? For example, does your software and hardware combination permit the full eighty columns of information to appear on the monitor as it would on a sheet of eight-and-one-half-inch by eleven-inch paper? (This factor may be dependent on hardware as well as software.)

- Is the word processor menu driven so that most processes are self-prompting and easily executed?
- How many lines appear on the screen?
- What are its formatting capabilities?
- Does it have special features, such as a built-in spelling checker, a mailing list utility, or a footnoting capability?
- What disc drive capacity does it require?

Word processing programs, more so than most other types of software, are heavily dependent on the hardware on which they are run. The first question to answer in considering hardware is whether to purchase a machine dedicated to word processing or to purchase one that can be used for tasks far removed from word processing as well. My bias is for the latter type of machine. If a piece of equipment is purchased that was not explicitly designed as a word processor, however, the purchaser must double check carefully its word processing capabilities. Questions such as the following are important considerations in choosing a computer when word processing is part of the planned usage:

- Does the computer generate a forty-column display, or is it possible to get an eighty-column display by means of added accessories?
- Is the keyboard well laid out? Is its design similar to that of a standard typewriter keyboard?
- Are there special function keys provided to facilitate the execution of special commands?
- What storage capacity do the disc drives have?
- Will the computer permit multitasking (that is, does the computer have the ability to perform more than one task at a time)? In word processing, the ability of a machine to prepare new text at the same time that previously prepared text is being printed out can be very important.
- Does the equipment have the ability to interface with other computers and related hardware?

Electronic Flip Chart or Slide Show — Computer Graphics

The term *graphics* refers to the use of lines and figures to display information on a computer monitor (Digital Corporation, 1982). The computer is uniquely well designed for display of information in a wide variety of forms. Letters, figures, and drawings created by the computer can be displayed in various configurations as points of light on a video monitor. Similarly, software can be designed to produce print of different sizes and styles as well as drawings and images.

Graphics Capabilities. Most often, computer graphics are prepared as files on discs that can be used in a fashion similar to slides prepared by a camera. An important advantage, however, is that no camera, development process, or enlargement equipment is required to produce a presentation that previously would have required using all that and more. The computer, with a monitor of sufficient resolution and size to be seen by the audience in question, can display these slides. In instances where it is not convenient or practical to use a computer and monitor, overhead transparencies of high quality can be produced from computer slides that have been printed out. The image produced is of greater readability than can be produced by a standard typewriter and would require special art work if not done by the computer.

Some graphics software packages provide the option of presenting a self-operating slide show, which can be used as an autotutorial or informational device similar to those used in airline terminals.

The integration of graphics capabilities with statistical programs permits data to be output in easy-to-read bar, line, and pie graph displays. Such information can then be easily incorporated into an electronic slide presentation.

As is the case with word processing and computer communications, the utility of graphics software lies in its enhancement of communication. While word processing and communication media are directed at written communication taking place in a noninteractive mode, graphics communication usually takes place with the communicator or presenter there in person. Just as illustrations in a book enhance written communication, graphics illustrations accompanying a spoken presentation enhance the spoken communication.

Student Development Applications. There are numerous areas in student development where graphics capabilities can enhance communication. If a student development officer is fortunate enough to have a microcomputer in a conference room, it takes but a few minutes to put together illustrations that will highlight an informational presentation effectively. As indicated earlier, if the audience is too large for all to see a standard video monitor or if the facilities do not have a microcomputer available, graphics can be used in the preparation of standard overhead transparencies. Used in this manner, graphics can augment effectively a staff meeting presentation or a presentation to a small group of persons.

An application of computer graphics well suited to individual as well as group presentations is the self-paced slide show that can be prepared in advance and played back later. Such programs include timing options that advance "slides" at a user-determined pace. Descriptions of the services offered by a given office, instructions for registration, and many other processes can be presented in autotutorial form. When transmitted via cable to monitors located around a student center, for example, the system takes on the utility of monitors such as those found in airline terminals.

Graphics programs used in conjunction with word processing systems can also be used to illustrate in-house publications. The result can be an attractively illustrated campus newsletter or weekly bulletin. Graphics capabilities run the gamut from very elaborate software programs used for animation to software that simply relies on the recall of previously prepared illustrations and type fonts. A library of illustrations saved on disc can serve as a convenient means of illustrating many in-house publications.

Using computer graphics for drafting also holds potential for student affairs applications. The computerized drawing of three-dimensional structures and layouts is a general purpose microcomputer application developed by engineers and architects. This capability can be applied to proposed layouts for student residences, proposed renovations, and similar applications where visual communication of ideas is desirable.

Selection Factors. Consider the following factors in looking at graphics applications:

- Ease of use
- Editing features
- Compatibility of the files produced with other software packages.

Electronic Mail and Computer Communications

A general purpose microcomputer application that holds great potential for student development is that of computer communications. One type of computer communications, electronic mail, provides communication between microcomputers or terminal stations. Transfer of information is possible between stations under the same roof by direct wiring or between stations located far apart by means of telephone lines. Individuals can communicate to one or more persons who also have access to a microcomputer or a suitably equipped terminal. A portable computer equipped with a modem will permit remote review of and response to correspondence. Much routine office work can, in fact, be handled from thousands of miles away nearly as effectively as if the person were at his or her desk. If necessary, a roadside phone booth can serve as the connecting link.

Communications Software Capabilities. In addition to a micro-computer or other type of computer terminal, you need a device called a *modem* to interface with time-sharing systems and other similarly equipped computers. The term modem is drived from two words: modulate and demodulate. In simple terms, microcomputers produce digital signals that contain the information sent by the user. These signals must be modulated or converted into audio tones in order to be transmitted by telephone. When received, these modulated tones must be demodulated or converted back into a digital signal to be displayed on the host terminal.

Modems recognize signals based on established protocols. These signals can be sent to a computer by means of direct keyboard input or through software. Direct keyboard input can be complicated, and it requires more sophistication than many users wish to develop. Software programs, therefore, have been designed to facilitate this process. This software must be designed for a particular modem as well as a particular computer; thus, it is important to coordinate the purchase of software with the purchase of equipment.

Using communications software, a microcomputer can automatically answer a call or dial another system. It can "log on" the system (a term used to describe the way a computer identifies itself that is analogous to a person signing a guest book), and it can even address a particular subsection of a computer time-sharing data base system (for example, electronic mail). By executing certain commands, a micro-computer can capture on disc all or part of what is displayed on the monitor. In this way, long-distance rates and computer time charges are minimized. Information is captured by the receiving terminal at maximum speed and played back later at leisure when charges are not being incurred. Memos, drafts of manuscripts, and whole computer program listings can be transmitted in this way. Currently, speeds are limited to between 300 baud (about 60 words per minute) and 1200 baud (about 240 words per minute). It is likely that speeds will increase as technology improves.

Applications to Student Development. At first glance, you might wonder why all these capabilities are so important. After all, we already have the typewritten memo, mail service, and the telephone, which have long served us well in providing communication. The advantages of computer communication, however, are striking. How often are professionals exasperated by the amount of time consumed trying to track down people by phone? Using electronic mail, you can forward memos at the speed of a telephone call but without the necessity of the recipient being present to receive them. Both the speed of the telephone call and the utility of having the message in writing are maintained.

Even electronic mail between persons whose offices are separated by only a few feet can save time. Time needed to locate the recipient is saved, and persons using electronic mail report they find themselves becoming more economical in the use of words. Further, the idle chatter that accompanies some in-person and phone communication is reduced or eliminated. This advantage can, indeed, be a double-edged sword. For some, it can lead to loss of personalization. Used properly, however, electronic mail can lead to more effective use of time and more quality interpersonal interaction. Computer conferences utilizing this technology can take place on an ongoing basis among individuals who are widely dispersed. Colleagues can engage in discussions of important topics in a manner that allows them to read each other's comments and respond later at their convenience.

Another application of computer communications lies in the use of time-sharing services such as Educom (a consortium of nonprofit institutions), Compuserve (a trademark of the H. and R. Block Company), and The Source (a trademark of Readers' Digest Corporation). By means of services such as these, you can access centralized data bases that are maintained by widely separated individuals. The term *time sharing* simply refers to the fact that a number of persons are sharing time on a central computer. Reference information regarding topics such as innovative orientation programs, alcoholic beverage policies, student judicial policies, and various types of management information can be centrally stored and maintained. Electronic mail and communication among institutions by means of electronic bulletin boards can be established as well. Information of nearly any type that can be imagined can be stored and retrieved later by use of these services.

Selection Factors. Consider the following in looking at communications packages:
- Software compatibility with the computer and modem being used
- Security and password provisions
- Special features available.

Developmental Concerns

Now that you know some of the capabilities of general purpose software, you may be wondering what the significance of this is to student development. Is the profession apt to sell its philosophical soul to the long-feared technological threats of mechanization and impersonalization? How does the technological revolution, as epitomized by computers, relate to human development? Is the profession going to become expert at software development rather than at student development?

The answer to all these questions is that we will become what we become as a result of what we ourselves do, whether it be with or without computers. Without computers, however, it will probably take us longer. These devices should be used to avoid dull, repetitive, non-challenging roles. The speed, accuracy, and efficiency of computers should free student development professionals from these tasks, not lock them into these tasks.

Student development professionals have begun to focus on how they can use computers to facilitate achievement of developmental goals. Writing on the utility of data base management applications, Erwin and Tollefson (1982) describe several ways in which computer technology can assist in the achievement of Chickering's developmental vectors. For example, developmental information can be collected during orientation programs and used to identify student deficiencies, to match roommates according to interests, or to match students with opportunities for extracurricular involvement. The authors go on to show how vocationally undecided students can be placed in special counseling groups, career development workshops, and special advising sessions, all using information gleaned from data bases. Students can also be assisted in selecting values-clarification workshops. And, finally, a data base can be used to evaluate the effectiveness of developmental programs.

Gillespie (1983) goes beyond the idea of computers being used as substitutes for repetitive functions. He suggests that the next stage of computerization involves use of computers as tools to do things not previously possible. He feels that computers can become so integral a part of the system that the goals and structure of the whole system are changed. Data bases, electronic spread sheets, and word processors are all illustrative of Gillespie's points. They each save repetitive work, but, by virtue of their speed and capacity, they also permit data collection, analysis, and reporting not previously possible simply because of the magnitude of the task. And, finally, they each eventually become so important a function that the entire system changes to take the greater capabilities into account. For example, organizations can now act on complete information rather than inferring from partial information or acting on assumptions that actual data may later prove incorrect.

John Holland (1978) suggests that we will never have sufficient counseling resources to provide vocational guidance to everyone who could benefit from this service. It is possible, however, that we may eventually have sufficient numbers of computers and well-written software programs to achieve this goal. The personal computer has nearly infinite capacity to individualize instruction in ways never dreamed possible.

Writing in *Today* magazine, Carole Gerber (1983) describes what has been dubbed "information sickness" by the Trend Analysis Program of the American Council on Life Insurance. Many nontechnical people today are overwhelmed by the language and hardware of technology, on the one hand, while being overrun by an information explosion on the other. She suggests that some non-technically inclined people may simply choose not to understand complicated information.

The challenge for student development professionals is to become educated as to computer capabilities and to participate in their implementation, rather than allowing others to take the lead and impose their solutions on the profession.

John Naisbitt (1982) alludes to the rapid growth and proliferation of new information. Indeed, without the capabilities of technology, it is no longer possible to remain current in most fields, including that of student development. Gerber notes that technological change not only upsets people emotionally but also leaves many behind. Those left behind are unable to cope and, as a result, are susceptible to depression. The similarity between information sickness and what is popularly referred to as burnout is notable.

Summary

This discussion of general purpose software should in no way be considered exhaustive. There are many fine software programs that have not been described, and there are undoubtedly numerous applications to student development of the programs discussed that were not identified. The major purpose of this discussion was to illustrate potential applications of software and to stimulate ideas.

For the busy student affairs professional, there is likely to be a temptation to put off becoming acquainted with the capabilities of microcomputers. This is even more likely to be the case if the individual in question views microcomputers as a fad, if he or she is not technically oriented, or is concerned about the dangers of impersonalization that can result from use of computers. Microcomputers, however, are here to stay. They have great potential to further not only mechanistic tasks, but also to enable us better to apply our knowledge of student development. In many cases, without the capability of computers, it would be virtually impossible to manage the data involved. In a time when the profession of student affairs is beset by declining enrollments and fiscal uncertainty, and is viewed by some as an expensive frill, the capability of microcomputers can be valuable resources.

While general purpose application software is valuable for many applications, software designed specifically for student development applications is still highly desirable. There is software available that is designed specifically for such applications, but exactly how much is available and how it can be located is difficult to determine. At least one software clearinghouse, The Student Development Software Clearinghouse, is underway. Hopefully the profit motive will further stimulate those in the profession with programming skills to market well documented, user-friendly software. In the meantime, carefully selected general purpose software offers a reasonable alternative and a good way to begin learning about microcomputer capabilities. Persons interested in gaining more information regarding the Student Development Software Clearinghouse should contact the author at Western Connecticut State University.

The software which has been described has much potential for further application in student development. If the cautions and considerations noted during this discussion are heeded, users can avoid pitfalls that cause loss of effectiveness and productivity. If cautions are not heeded, however, time can be wasted and frustrations encountered. Microcomputers are not the answer to all our problems but simply another tool for our use. In each circumstance, we should ask whether our students and colleagues are better off with the use of computers than they are without.

References

Baldridge, V. Address to the American College Personnel Association, Houston, Texas, April 13, 1983.

Castlewitz, D., Chiasausky, L., and Kronberg, P. *Visicalc Home and Office Companion.* Berkeley, Calif.: Osborne/McGraw-Hill, 1982.

Digital Corporation. *Guide to Personal Computing.* Concord, Mass.: Digital Corporation, 1982.

Erwin, T., and Tollefson, A. "A Data Base Management Model for Student Development." *Journal of College Student Personnel,* 1982, *13* (1), 70–76.

Gerber, C. "Information Sickness: A Disease of the New Technology?" *Today,* 1983, *2* (10), 26.

Gillespie, R. "Computing and Higher Education: The Revolution is Through the Gates." *Forum for Liberal Education,* 1983, *5* (6), 2-8.

Holland, J. In J. Whiteley (Ed.), *Career Counseling.* Monterey, Calif.: Brooks/Cole, 1978.

Naisbitt, J. *Megatrends.* New York: Warner, 1982.

L. Russell Watjen is dean of student affairs at Western Connecticut State University, and is responsible for a student affairs software clearinghouse for the American College Personnel Association.

*Professionals in student development are presented with the
dilemma of finding the computer useful for solving a variety
of information processing problems, while they also discover
that a host of ethical problems can result from misuse of
computer applications.*

Ethical Considerations
in Computer Use

James P. Sampson, Jr.

Drastic reductions in the cost and complexity of computer hardware
and software have greatly expanded the use of computers in providing
student services. There are few, if any, areas in student development
that are not dependent on computer applications to some extent. Computer technology has improved existing services and at the same time
has made new, previously unavailable services possible. New computer
applications continue to flourish in spite of the problems that have been
encountered in the design and implementation of these systems.

Ethical problems related to misuse of student information and
student services have existed for some time. Now, with the advent of
computer applications in student development some additional problems have been created. This chapter identifies the ways in which computer applications create these potential ethical problems, presents
ethical principles designed to minimize problems, and discusses the
responsibilities of professional organizations, academic departments
involved in preservice training, commercial system developers, and
institutions using computer applications.

C. S. Johnson, K. R. Pyle (Eds.). *Enhancing Student Development with Computers.*
New Directions for Student Services, no. 26. San Francisco: Jossey-Bass, June 1984.

Current Status of Computers in Student Development

Computer use in student development can be categorized into two groups. The first group of applications, which are provided by student development staff members, involves providing services to students. Examples include admissions, registration, and financial aid systems. The second group of applications involves students use of the computer to obtain direct services. Examples include career guidance, counseling, and testing systems. Computers are used in both of these situations because of their superior data processing capabilities in comparison to that of humans, and they thus free the student development staff member to spend more time in interpersonal tasks that are better suited to their abilities.

Potential ethical problems emerge, however, when traditional information processing functions are transferred from student development staff members to the computer. While staff members may not be needed actually to complete certain information processing tasks, staff members still need to supervise the process. If they fail to supervise the use of computer applications, then instances of inappropriate access to services and sensitive data will undoubtedly increase.

As other authors in this sourcebook have described, computer applications in student development were limited initially to large data processing operations such as registration. Such applications used large mainframe computers that required sophisticated programming staff for operation. The recent availability of microcomputers has greatly increased the computing power directly available to students and professional staff because, in comparison to mainframe computers, microcomputers can be operated without knowledge of advanced programming languages. As a result, all areas of student development can use computer applications to some extent. But this increased availability of computing power can be a problem as well as a blessing. Less restricted access to computer applications makes it potentially easier to use this resource in an inappropriate manner.

Another important trend involves the interconnection of a variety of microcomputers and mainframes at an institution. This approach, which is referred to as *distributed processing,* enables the user to match the data processing requirements of a particular program to the computer of the appropriate size. For example, word processing is most cost effective on a microcomputer, while accessing the academic records of all students at a large institution is most cost effective on a mainframe computer. Most student development tasks can be completed adequately by a microcomputer, but distributed processing allows you to access a mainframe computer, using the microcomputer as a terminal when the microcomputer is incapable of completing the job. The advantages of interconnecting computers through distributed processing are negated, however, when unauthorized users at remote locations on campus gain access to restricted data and services.

The use of computer networks comprises still another important trend. Computer networks allow the user, via telephone lines or satellite, to access data files, programs, or specialized computational procedures on a computer that may be located almost anywhere. This greatly expands the data processing capabilities of any single institution. But the potential problems of unauthorized computer access are multiplied when data and services can be accessed from almost anywhere through a computer network.

Our profession has not been unaware of the potential ethical problems associated with computer use. Some years ago, Lister (1970), Godwin and Bode (1971), and Super (1973) identified many of the basic issues. At this point, however, a clear consensus on how to deal effectively with these problems does not exist. At present, the "Statement of Ethical and Professional Standards," (American College Personnel Association, 1981), the *Ethical Standards* (American Personnel and Guidance Association, 1981), and the "Ethical Principles of Psychologists" (American Psychological Association, 1981) do not deal specifically with the problems associated with computer applications. In view of this situation, student development professionals must take an active part in formulating institutional standards that minimize ethical problems, as well as in providing input to professional associations for the modification of existing ethical principles. The following sections examine some specific ethical problems.

Confidentiality of Student Records

Institutions of higher education maintain substantial amounts of data on students. Some student information, such as residence hall assignment or participation in student activities, is not sensitive in nature, but other information, such as medical or counseling records, is considered quite sensitive. To understand how sensitive data can be a problem in computer-assisted record-keeping systems, we must review how the process of maintaining records has changed because of computer technology.

In traditional manual record-keeping systems, physical space is a consistent problem, and thus the amount of data that can be maintained on any one student is restricted. Also, as students are added to the record-keeping system, older student data must be removed to provide needed space. Computer technology has changed all of this. Now, mass storage devices such as computer discs and tapes can maintain vast amounts of data cost-effectively. The constraints of space, which tended to limit data collection to the essentials, have been greatly reduced (Gambrell and Sandfield, 1979; Lister, 1970). As a result, large quantities of information can be maintained on any one student.

Without careful management, student record-keeping systems can grow to the point that a great deal of unnecessary information is being collected. A related problem exists where increased data storage capacity makes it possible to keep student information for an almost unlimited amount of time (Gambrell and Sandfield, 1979). For example, out-of-date test results may be maintained even though the information is no longer relevant to providing services. When large amounts of data are maintained for long periods of time, the potential for misuse increases substantially.

In both manual and computerized record-keeping systems, data are often transferred from an original data collection form, such as a questionnaire, to a final document, such as a report. In the process of transferring the data, mistakes are inevitable. Inaccurate information can cause substantial problems for both staff and students. Lister (1970) pointed out that errors made with computer systems may be potentially more damaging in comparison to those of traditional systems because of the general public perception that computer data are somehow more valuable and reliable.

In a traditional student information system, the data can only be accessed where it is stored. For example, counseling records are only accessible at the counseling center. In a computerized record-keeping system, data may be accessed from a variety of computer terminals and microcomputers around the campus. The ease of access that exists with distributed processing becomes a potential liability when sensitive data can be obtained by unauthorized individuals. This situation has prompted some professionals to recommend that sensitive data be excluded from computerized systems (Denkowski and Denkowski, 1982). As we become more and more dependent on computerized record keeping, this may not be feasible.

The standard approach to solving this problem has been to protect files with one or more passwords. Although this can be effective, experience suggests that passwords are not changed frequently enough and are very easy to obtain. Careful attention to password security and to locking up microcomputer data storage diskettes physically can provide at least partial protection.

The problem described above can be further complicated when sensitive data can be accessed through computer networks. The Ad Hoc Committee on Ethical Standards in Psychological Research (1973) states that confidentiality can be violated when information in data banks can be associated with specific individuals.

One further problem that generally is not associated with traditional record-keeping systems concerns the capability of some computerized systems to collect data without the knowledge of the user. For example, research data can be collected while students use some types of computer-assisted career guidance systems. Obvious ethical problems can result if these data are collected without the informed consent of the student.

Sampson and Pyle (1983) suggest the following ethical principles to minimize the problems associated with confidentiality of student records:

1. Ensure that confidential data maintained on a computer are limited to information that is appropriate and necessary for the services being provided.

2. Ensure that confidential data maintained on a computer are destroyed after it is determined that the information is no longer of any value in providing services.

3. Ensure that confidential data maintained on a computer are accurate and complete.

4. Ensure that access to confidential data is restricted to appropriate professionals by using the best computer security methods available (*appropriate professionals* is a term described in existing ethical standards).

5. Ensure that it is not possible to identify with any particular individual confidential data maintained in a computerized data bank that is accessible through a computer network.

6. Ensure that research participation release forms are completed by any individual who has automatically collected individually identifiable data as a result of using a computer-assisted counseling, testing, or guidance system.

Applications in Computer-Assisted Testing and Assessment

Many student development functions include testing and assessment as a component of providing services. Most of the tasks associated with testing in counseling, career guidance, placement, admissions, and academic advisement are repetitive, clerical, and computational in nature. The computer is especially well suited to test administration, scoring, and profile generation, thus giving staff members more time to assist students in applying test results to specific situations. A related innovation involves the use of microcomputer-controlled generalized test interpretations. "Clients who view a generalized interpretation of test results can improve their preparation for counseling by being aware of basic terminology, concepts, and the general nature of their scores" (Sampson, 1983, p. 294). After viewing a generalized interpretation, the student completes an individual or group session with a staff member to discuss his or her results.

In comparison with traditional testing and assessment practices, the computerized approach offers many advantages. Some unique problems also exist, however. When a staff member makes an error in administrating, scoring, or interpreting a test, the potential for harm is generally limited to only one individual. On the other hand, if such an error is made by a computer, many students may be harmed before the problem is detected. A similar difficulty can arise when students reach erroneous conclusions about test results after they view a generalized test interpretation developed by someone who does not fully understand the instrument being used.

The following ethical principles may help to minimize some of these problems (Sampson and Pyle, 1983).

1. Ensure that computer-controlled test scoring equipment and programs function properly, thereby providing individuals with accurate test results.

2. Ensure that generalized interpretations of test results presented by microcomputer-controlled audiovisual devices accurately reflect the intention of the test author.

Counselor Intervention

Prior to the advent of computer applications, the process of providing student services was conducted by staff members. For example, if a student sought career counseling, a counselor would provide assistance in assessment and help in identifying occupational alternatives, obtaining informaton, and formulating a decision-making strategy. This process has changed. Many of the repetitive clerical, computational, instructional, and information-dissemination tasks are now completed by the computer. The counselor then deals with the more interpersonal aspects of the helping process as well as with tasks that are beyond the capacity of the computer. This approach has been effective because both human and machine are used for tasks that are suited to their unique abilities.

The transition has created some problems. It is now possible for a student to receive a wide variety of services with little or no contact with a counselor. The question arises as to how much and what type of counselor intervention is necessary. Students do seem to need to have contact with a staff member at various times while they complete a computer-assisted career guidance system. Sampson and Stipling (1979) found that students preferred a structured counselor intervention approach, consisting of a systematic introduction to and follow-up of computer use, over a nonstructured approach. A majority of students who did not see a counselor before or during their use of the computer planned to schedule a follow-up counseling appointment. Pyle and Stripling (1976) found that the career maturity of students was increased when a computer-assisted career guidance system was completed with counselor assistance. When a counselor was not involved in the system, Devine (1975) found that no changes in career maturity occurred.

Counselors are still needed in the provision of counseling services because they perform functions that are beyond the capacity of present computers. For example, a student who is having difficulty maintaining adequate motivation to study may decide that a change in major is needed and may attempt to solve his or her problem by using a computer-assisted career guidance system available at a counseling center. The computer systems presently available are not able to identify other issues, such as emotional, family, or financial difficulties, that may be more germane to the problem than the choice of major. This task, then, can only be dealt with adequately by a counselor. The amount and type of counselor intervention necessary depends on the students' needs and the nature of the computer application being used.

When inadequate counselor intervention is provided for students who use computer-assisted counseling, testing, and guidance systems, a variety of problems may result. Some students seek counseling services at a time when they are experiencing acute emotional problems. Individuals in a crisis situation are generally unable to use a computer effectively. Systematic prescreening prior to computer use is needed to identify such individuals, so that other more appropriate counseling resources can be used.

It is common for students to have inappropriate expectations of a computer application. Also, students may worry that they will be unable to make the system function properly or that they will make an error and damage the hardware or software in some way; such anxiety severely limits the student's ability to use the system effectively. A related problem is that students may misunderstand the purpose and operation of the computer application. As a result, the student may become frustrated and fail to complete the process, or may complete the process but draw erroneous conclusions about the results. For example, a student may believe that the computer is capable of completely solving his or her problem.

If a follow-up of a student's use of a computer application is not provided, then potential problems related to inappropriate use of the system or misunderstandings about the results may not be identifiable and corrected. The subsequent needs of the student after completion of the computer application may not be discussed if a counselor follow-up is not part of the process.

Two final problems may occur if a staff member is not involved in students' use of computer applications. First, the occupational and educational information contained in computer-assisted career guidance systems is drawn from a variety of national and local sources. Both the quality of this information and its applicability to local situations vary. Without staff intervention to rectify potential problems in the data base, students may draw erroneous conclusions from information in the system. Second, the hardware and software that operate various computer applications may fail to function properly, resulting in student anxiety and frustration. Without staff intervention to correct these difficulties or to recommend other resources, frustration may prompt students to discontinue the counseling process.

Sampson and Pyle (1983) suggest the following ethical principles:

1. Ensure that a client's needs are assessed to determine if using a particular computer-assisted system is appropriate.

2. Ensure that an introduction to using a computer-assisted counseling, testing, or guidance system is available to reduce possible anxiety concerning the system, misconceptions about the role of the computer, and misunderstandings about basic concepts or about the operation of the system.

3. Ensure that a follow-up activity to using a computer-assisted counseling, testing, or guidance system is available to correct possible misconceptions, misunderstandings, or inappropriate use as well as to assess subsequent needs of the client.

4. Ensure that the information contained in a computer-assisted career counseling and guidance system is accurate and up to date.

5. Ensure that the equipment and programs that operate a computer-assisted counseling, testing, and guidance system function properly.

6. The need for counselor intervention depends on the likelihood that the client will experience difficulties that will in turn limit the effectiveness of the system or otherwise exacerbate the client's problem. It is the counselor's responsibility to decide whether the best approach to avoiding these problems for a specific client population is direct intervention or indirect intervention through the use of workbooks, self-help guides, or other exercises. In general, academic counseling systems and career guidance systems that primarily provide information can be used effectively with less direct counselor intervention than personal counseling, testing and assessment systems, or career guidance systems that provide assessment and guidance functions. In spite of the fact that some academic and career systems may need less direct counselor intervention, the individuals who use these systems can still benefit from direct intervention when counselors are available.

Priorities for Action

Unethical use of computer applications in student development settings is a complex problem. A coordinated effort among profesional organizations, academic departments involved in preservice training, commercial system developers, and institutions using computer applications is needed to reduce the chances that these applications will be used inappropriately.

Professional organizations need to: (1) revise existing ethical statements and standards for preservice training to include issues related to computer applications and (2) provide in-service training in the area of computer applications.

Academic departments involved in preservice training need to: (1) include problems related to ethical use of computer applications in professional issues and ethics courses and (2) require students in practicum and internship placements to explore the ethical issues related to the use of computer technology in their setting.

Commercial system developers need to: (1) provide documentation on field testing of computer applications to those interested in purchasing the system and (2) provide field-tested training materials and suggested implementation strategies with the purchase of a computer system.

Institutions using computer applications need to: (1) conduct in-service training in the area of general computer literacy and the use of specific systems and (2) monitor computer applications to ensure that the systems are used in an ethical manner.

Summary

The basic goals for providing services to students in higher education have not changed, but the infusion of computer technology into higher education has changed the manner in which services are delivered. Previous methods used to ensure confidentiality of student records and appropriate use of counseling, testing, and guidance resources are inadequate to deal with the unique problems resulting from the use of computer applications. To reduce ethical problems, both professionals and the profession at large must become aware of the issues involved and take concrete actions to prevent abuse.

References

Ad Hoc Committee on Ethical Standards in Psychological Research. *Ethical Principles in the Conduct of Research with Human Participants.* Washington, D.C.: American Psychological Association, 1973.

American College Personnel Association. "Statement of Ethical and Professional Standards." *Journal of College Student Personnel,* 1981, *22,* 184–189.

American Personnel and Guidance Association. *Ethical Standards.* Washington, D.C.: American Personnel and Guidance Association, 1981.

American Psychological Association. "Ethical Principles of Psychologists." *American Psychologist,* 1981, *36,* 633–638.

Denkowski, K. M., and Denkowski, G. C. "Client-Counselor Confidentiality: An Update of Rationale, Legal Status, and Implications." *Personnel and Guidance Journal,* 1982, *60,* 371–375.

Devine, H. F. "The Effects of a Computer-Assisted Career Counseling Program on the Vocational Maturity of Community College Students." Unpublished doctoral dissertation, University of Florida, Gainesville, 1975.

Gambrell, J. B., and Sandfield, R. E. "Computers in the Schools: Too Much Too Soon?" *High School Journal,* 1979, *68,* 327–331.

Godwin, W. F., and Bode, K. A. "Privacy and the New Technology." *Personnel and Guidance Journal,* 1971, *50,* 298–304.

Lister, C. "Privacy and Large-Scale Data Systems." *Personnel and Guidance Journal,* 1970, *49,* 207–211.

Pyle, K. R., and Stripling, R. O. "The Counselor, the Computer, and Career Development." *Vocational Guidance Quarterly,* 1976, *25,* 71–75.

Sampson, J. P., Jr. "Computer-Assisted Testing and Assessment: Current Status and Implications for the Future." *Measurement and Evaluation in Guidance,* 1983, *15,* 293–299.

Sampson, J. P., Jr., and Pyle, K. R. "Ethical Issues Involved with the Use of Computer-Assisted Counseling, Testing, and Guidance Systems." *Personnel and Guidance Journal,* 1983, *61,* 283–287.

Sampson, J. P., Jr., and Stripling, R. O. "Strategies for Counselor Intervention with a Computer-Assisted Career Guidance System." *Vocational Guidance Quarterly,* 1979, *27,* 230–238.

Super, D. E. "Computers in Support of Vocational Development and Counseling." In H. Borow (Ed.), *Career Guidance for a New Age.* Boston: Houghton Mifflin, 1973.

James P. Sampson, Jr., is an assistant professor in the Department of Human Services and Studies at Florida State University in Tallahassee, Florida.

How effective student development educators are in the
high-technology age of the future will largely depend
upon our vision.

The Future:
Creating the Vision

K. Richard Pyle

History tells us that 200 years went by after the book was introduced
before it was used by teachers (Norris, 1982). Does such a fate exist for
the computer? Among predictions on computers in higher education as
reported by the *Chronicle of Higher Education* (1983) were these:

- There will be twenty times more microcomputers in use on
  American campuses in 1985 than there were in 1980.
- Within twenty years, computers will have replaced the book
  as the major delivery device in bringing education to
  students.
- Personal microcomputers will increase the scholar's freedom
  from centralized bureaucracy by allowing individual control
  of the technology and direct access to widely dispersed
  sources of information.

Citing a survey by a marketing research company, Theodore
Ricks (1983) estimates that the average number of microcomputers per
college has increased from six in 1980 to forty-five in 1983 and is expected to grow to 141 in 1985. In addition, the power of the microcomputer appears to be increasing dramatically while the cost will
remain approximately the same. It is estimated that there will continue

C. S. Johnson, K. R. Pyle (Eds.) *Enhancing Student Development with Computers.*
New Directions for Student Services, no. 26. San Francisco: Jossey-Bass, June 1984.

to be a doubling of computer power every two years. This means that within ten years computers will be approximately thirty times more powerful than the ones that are in use today (Lipson, 1980).

"A person who has a personal computer does not have to stand in line or walk across the campus to use it," notes John Strange (1983, p. 9), a professor in the College of Public and Community Services of the University of Massachusetts. That is one of the reasons, he says, that "personal computers can be expected to have a greater impact on higher education than other new technology." Mr. Strange adds that "the speed with which microcomputer technology will spread through higher education will be underestimated by most of us. The decentralizing of knowledge through the use of microcomputers has the potential of affecting traditional hierarchies on campus so that deans may know things sooner than the vice-chancellor."

Gillespie (1983) views the integration of computers in higher education as a three-stage sequence. The first step is that in which "computers" are used as replacements for functions performed manually. Secondly, computers become tools for new kinds of tasks as new capabilities are found. Thirdly, computers will become structurally integrated into the system, forcing reanalysis of goals and overall structure (p. 3).

Ross (1982), synthesizing the work of authors reporting on future issues in student development, counseling, and guidance, concludes that the impact of electronic communication and computing cannot be underestimated: "We will be living in an 'intelligent' environment, having extensive and constant contact with computers and telecommunication devices. The marketplace will become customized rather than mass produced, courtesy of computers. We will have the capacity to be instantly in communication with persons throughout the world. Offices will have the capacity to eliminate the use of paper, relying on electronic mail and storage. Becuase of changes in both hardware and software, it will become *easier* for the average person to use computers" (p. 2).

Such information supports the idea that the computer will be heavily used. The critical questions are how will it be used and whether its use will really change education in ways that are positive and growth producing.

Education in the Future

Alvin Toffler (1980) views American education as obsolete; it produces people who fit into a reasonably well-functioning industrial society but, unfortunately, we no longer have such a society. As schools shift away from the industrial model, they will have to turn out a different kind of person. Toffler is convinced that what is really needed is to produce people who can cope with change.

Such a educational goal appears to fall within the framework not of the academicians who are working toward cognitive development but of student development educators — people who are trained and committed to assisting people in coping more effectively with their environment. To be successful, we will need to use all the tools that are available to us to their fullest potential.

Student Development in the Future

Toffler maintains that there are two popular, contrasting views of the future. One view expects the future to continue the trends now evident. This straight-line thinking has been severely shaken by news of crisis after crisis. Thus, a bleaker version has become increasingly popular, and many people believe that today's society has no future. Both views produce the same results: Both lead to the paralysis of imagination and will.

John Naisbitt (1982) says we are living in a time of parenthesis, the time between eras. "In stable eras, everything has a name and everything knows its place, and we can leverage very little. But in the time of parenthesis we have extraordinary leverage and influence — individually, professionally, and institutionally — if we can only get a clear sense, a clear conception, a clear vision of the road ahead" (p. 252).

The first step, therefore, in successfully designing a desirable future is to believe that it can be done. The *Aquarian Conspiracy* (Ferguson, 1980) promotes the idea of the autonomous individual in a decentralized society. These advocates are people who are experiencing a growing capacity for change in themselves and know that it is possible for others. Such an approach has always been a major principle of student development, but now student development has a major transformation movement on its side. We are now in a position to influence the future.

Enhancing Development

As we consider the developmental potential of computers, a three-stage model is proposed to help us in our thinking. Each stage relates to material already discussed in this sourcebook.

In stage one, the computer is used for information retrieval and essentially as an extension of a book. Many of the computer-assisted career information systems described in Chapter One relate to this stage. Basically, the computer is used here for quick access to information.

Stage two involves using the computer in administrative ways. Chapter Five discusses many of the administrative applications. In this context, we are not only getting information from the computer but also having it perform a type of data manipulation. Thus, it extends our skill level. Examples of these applications are word processing, electronic spread sheets, and accounting programs.

Stage three is the use of the computer in developing cognitive skills and as a teaching tool. At this level, we are using the computer to help us think through possibilities, to give us feedback on our thinking, and to help us see possibilities and alternatives not previously known. Programs at this level focus on developing higher levels of thinking, understanding, and reflection. Some of the programs discussed in Chapter One fall into this category. They include the computer-assisted guidance programs of DISCOVER and SIGI, the PLATO DCS counseling programs, and the developmental work to assist adults in their lifelong learning being developed by the Educational Testing Service and the American College Testing Program.

The real challenge for student development educators lies in stage three. At this time, there are not many programs available that help accomplish the goals of this stage. Two examples of teaching tools with developmental possibilities are:

1. Using Erikson's (1959) stages, a student might determine where he or she is in each of the stage continuums. With the computer providing relevant examples, an adolescent might practice assessing where one fits into the identity stage and then attempt to do the same for himself or herself. A similar process could be used with Chickering's (1972) vectors and Perry's (1970) stages. The creator of such a program would need to think of creative ways of presenting the information. Critical incidents and case studies are approaches that can be used to help people apply the theory to practical situations.

2. Kohlberg's (1972) theory of moral development could be turned into a game where the computer provides forced-choice scenarios requiring a decision with moral implications. Feedback using Kohlberg's theory on each of the decisions made would provide the opportunity to teach the user what each of the levels means. The user could add his or her own situations with a decision, either real or imagined, in order to develop a clearer idea of the model.

Such programs must be based on the assumption that people can intentionally work toward their own psychological development by applying experience to supported developmental theories. The computer would be used to help the individual both understand the theory and move toward a higher level of psychological integration and awareness.

High Tech/High Touch

Much has been said recently about the need to move aggressively into the technological age while heightening sensitivity to our humanity and our affective needs. If we are to do this, student development educators need to know where computers can be used most effectively and where human contact cannot be replaced by a machine. What are the areas where human contact is most critical? Where does the computer leave off and the human begin? We need a model to develop research questions and find answers.

Christopher Dede (1981) of the University of Houston has proposed that, in the instructional process, there are many content areas that lend themselves to computer use. Dede suggests that teachers will use the machine to teach basic content and subject matter with a limited range of right answers. Such subjects as reading, basic mathematics, accounting, and so on will be taught by computers, while education in creative writing, clinical psychology, ethnography, and so on will continue to be achieved by teachers. The machine might be capable of handling instructional units that involve multiple "right answers," but the difficulties and costs are prohibitive compared to using human teachers. Thus, the involvement of the human is contingent upon costs and difficulty. Dede foresees the present curriculum being taught in a third of the time it takes currently. This will allow both financial savings and the potential for students to move along faster in the development of their cognitive skills.

Applying Dede's thinking to student development, we can see that the computer might accomplish such basic administrative tasks as report and letter writing, data analysis, filing and maintaining information systems and accountability logs. Other areas in which the computer might be of assistance are in basic skill development (such as study skills), in tutoring assistance on basic subject matters, and in resumé development. However, if Dede's prognosis is correct, economic factors will largely prevent us from developing elaborate multiple-right-answer systems. These might include such decision-making activities as resolving a personal problem with a number of variables that are difficult to put into perspective.

A model of overlapping concentric circles is proposed to help guide our thinking in making the high tech/high touch distinction. Where the circles overlap can be considered the areas where human contact along with the machine can be of greatest value. Let us call this area two. The first circle, area one, would be the content that can be handled by the computer alone. Included would be information we attempt to communicate to students during orientation and the information in the college catalogue. Students could access the computer at a variety of places on campus to gain information on questions such as rules and regulations, financial aid procedures, services available and how to use them, and where to get help for any specific question. In addition, the first circle would include administrative applications such as roommate pairings, financial needs analyses, data bases, and automated admissions decisions.

Area two, where the machine and human appear to be most effective when used in conjunction, includes computer-assisted guidance programs as a laboratory experience for students in a career development class and small-group or individual counseling. This area would also include any content that requires processing and integrating as well as depth of thinking and reflection.

In area three are those multiple-answer activities for which the machine is not equipped. Counseling students on emotional and psychological concerns, problem solving on matters that go beyond the computer programming capacity, and areas that require human contact due to the unique nature of the human interaction are examples of such activities.

Research is needed to help student development educators identify appropriately what functions can best be achieved by the computer (area one), by counselor and computer (area two), and by counselor alone (area three).

Life as a Student Development Educator in the Year 2000

Although future forecasters admit to the difficulty of making long-range predictions (beyond five years), there are certainly trends that provide insight into what we can expect. The scenario that follows is a positive one and is based on the assumption that world conditions will remain stable and that student development professionals will take an assertive role in the use of computer technology.

Computer Usage. Student development professionals will have access to and be a part of an integrated computer center where communication will take place with ease among colleagues and other educators.

Comprehensive data bases will make it easy to gain information on a variety of subjects and activities. For example, student profiles will be instantly available, providing student development educators with the latest update on students. These profiles will not only include demographic information but also developmental levels and needs along with personality information such as learning styles, interests, values, temperament, and skills. Not only will such information be descriptive but it will also be prescriptive, with the computer suggesting and outlining potential interventions for the educator to consider in assisting the student.

Telecomputing will make it easy for us to communicate with colleagues and thus increase access to the most recent program ideas and research findings. Computers will be able to talk to one another through networks. Consequently, professional journals as we now know them will not exist. Such information will come to us via the electronic medium and be updated on a daily basis as professionals and graduate students enter into the computer their research findings and activities. There will be a grading and an editing of these works, but they will not have to be delivered through a monthly or quarterly publication. Professionally certified bulletin boards will be the vehicle by which information will be accessed with professions and institutions charged hook-up time or a flat rate per hour of use. More of us will find it possible to do our work at home because of the power of telecomputing. Time spent with students and colleagues will be on those matters that require a high level of human interaction and on problems that are hard to pinpoint and are abstract in nature.

Roles and Functions. Due to the ease of communication and the sending out of reports and letters through talking into the computer (the computer will be able to translate our words into type), we will no longer need the traditional secretary or clerical worker. The computer will automatically file information for us. In place of secretaries will be paraprofessionals who will be trained to handle problem-solving matters that are not economical for the computer to handle. These individuals will be graduate students and entering professionals who have been trained and certified on their interpersonal communication skills. They will also be trained to determine and design, with computer assistance, special programs and interventions that have proved successful with a variety of developmental needs.

In place of the present hierarchical management and administrative organization, we will find more of a consultative and wandering form of supervision. Educators will have specific developmental tasks to achieve and will become competent in a specialty area. These areas will fall more into line with students' developmental needs than with an administrative construct. For example, instead of student activity administrators, we will have social development specialists. Instead of financial aid counselors, we will have individuals trained in assisting students in developing instrumental autonomy. Such a staff will be task oriented and will use their supervisors in a consultative capacity to help them achieve their tasks. Computers will help us to be more accountable and objective, and this, in turn, will cut down on the need to be political to accomplish a goal or task. Supervising will not have to be highly structured since results will be on the computer and can be easily documented. This will free the supervisor to work more on interpersonal levels rather than on a task-management level. This movement in and out of informal contact is called a wandering form of supervision.

Populations. The word *student* will be one that will fit all of us who are in some way attempting to improve ourselves in an intentional manner. Therefore, the stereotype of the student falling into the age range from six to twenty-two will disappear. We will find that individuals will be highly involved as students or learners all of their lives. Adults of all ages will access curricula and seek assistance in their development in such increasing numbers that by the year 2000, the present-day distinctions of traditional-age student and nontraditional student will be completely broken down. Therefore, we will work regularly with people of all ages and cultures. We will find increasing activity by the year 2000 with individuals in other nations. This will help to bring about increased sensitivity and awareness of other cultures and their uniqueness. As Jean Houston (1982) has prophesied, there will be the "knows and the know nots" as opposed to the "haves and have nots."

Distance counseling and education will be available for individuals in remote areas through the telecommunications media. A network of educators and counselors will be available to people in these remote areas to help them with particular problems and with synthesis of information.

Curricula. Our curricula will be directed at helping students with life management and life-style skills. Such areas as helping people learn how to learn, how to cope with change, and how to parent will be commonplace. In addition, we will be working more with faculty in a consultative capacity to aid them in understanding learning styles and the impact that teaching modes have on students. Faculty, of course, will only teach those higher-level cognitive skills — for example, creative writing versus basic math.

In addition, the holistic health and spiritual dimensions will be more highly attended to with a variety of rich experiential opportunities available to aid people in their development in these areas. Experiential learning will be a critical ingredient and consume a lot of time, since cognitive development will be enhanced and accomplished in greater efficiency with the computer. As a consequence, student development educators will be individuals who are highly trained and skilled in experiential learning and in its impact on psychological and social development. Many of us will be known as experiential learning specialists, and we will influence curricular design through our knowledge and skills in this area.

Negative Aspects of Computers in Student Development

The potential dangers and pitfalls of computer misuse must also be addressed. As is true of any new tool, if the computer is not properly used, harm can be done. The early years of developmental testing show how misuse occurred when educators rushed to the testing bandwagon. We still hear students asking to take a test so they can find out once and for all what they are supposed to do with their lives.

In today's society, it is not uncommon for the computer to be anthropomorphized. We hear such statements as "the computer told me that this was the problem" or "that's what the computer said." It is easy for people to place so much faith in the computer that they forget that it was programmed and developed by fallible human beings.

Coburn (1982) points out that we should be sensitive to: (1) the potential decline in necessary computational skills as computers handle more and more of our daily uses of numbers; (2) an erosion of the print-based culture on which schools are based as more time is spent with computers and less with books and magazines; and (3) the new and greater pressures on schools to provide equal opportunity in a society in which computers are likely to widen the gap between the rich and the poor, the powerful and the powerless.

Education is known as a fad-conscious profession. In recent years, educators have gone through such movements as values clarification, career education, modern math, and back-to-basics. It might be easy for our fad-oriented profession to jump on the computer bandwagon too quickly, assuming that it is a solver of our problems. We need to keep in mind that the aimlessness of everyday life experienced by millions in modern society has deep roots in the individual alienation from nature, from work, and from other human beings. Weizenbaum (1979) states that "no fix, technological or otherwise, of the American education system that does not recognize that American schools are rapidly becoming America's principal juvenile mimimum security prisons can be expected to have socially therapeutic effects" (p. 440). Applying that to higher education and student development, we have to keep in mind the realities of what a human being can do that a computer cannot.

Questions We Need to Address

There is no question that computers have helped and can continue to help us accomplish the goals of student development. There are important questions that we in student development must keep in mind and ask, however, as we enter the technological age. Some of these questions are almost never asked—for example, who is the beneficiary of our much-advertised technological progress, and who are its victims? What limits should we, the people in general, and scientists and engineers in particular, impose on the application of computers to human affairs? What is the impact of the computer, not only on the economies of the world or on the war potential of nations but also on the self-image of human beings or on human dignity? What irreversible forces are our worship of high technology, symbolized most starkly by the computer, bringing into play? Will our children be able to live with the world we are constructing? What role will student/human development professionals play in helping to resolve these questions on the side of human dignity and growth to bring about a world of peace and human fulfillment?

These are global questions; the more pragmatic and day-to-day questions we need to address are also critical. These include what changes in present management structures will be necessary to protect the student from potential misuse of the computer. Will we need to carve out a role for a new student development specialist who is skilled and competent in computer knowledge and use? What systems will best bring about the full potential of the computer and student? How can we best integrate the machine with the human? What are the ethical considerations that need to be taken into consideration as we use the computer in areas such as counseling, skill building, and decision making?

Potential Role for the Student Development Educator

Joseph Lipson (1980) of the National Science Foundation provides student development educators with a vision of their role in the future: "I would propose that to realize the full potential of the computer we will need a richer vision of human development and human learning. I would also propose that we need to more fully grasp the nature and power of the computer as an extension of human intelligence. Only then will we be able to design learning environments that orchestrate the fantastic range of possibilities that the new technologies have opened for us. We will need imagination and talent as well as a sense of the indispensible role that human interaction should play" (p. 152).

Who else but student development educators can take up such a challenge? We often contend that we are the profession that strives to create higher levels of development and learning while grounding our philosophy in human interaction. The potential is there; how will we react to it?

References

Chickering, A. W. *Education and Identity.* San Francisco: Jossey-Bass, 1972.

Coburn, D. W. *Practical Guide to Computers in Education.* Reading, Mass.: Addison-Wesley, 1982.

Dede, C. "Educational, Social, and Ethical Implications of Technological Innovation." *Programmed Learning and Educational Technology,* 1981, *18* (4), 204–123.

Erikson, E. H. "Identity and the Life Cycle." *Psychological Issues Monograph,* 1959, *1* (1).

Ferguson, M. *The Aquarian Conspiracy.* Los Angeles: Jarcha, 1980.

Gillespie, R. "Computing and Higher Education: The Revolution Is Through the Gates." *Forum for Liberal Education,* 1983, *5* (6), 2–8.

Houston, J. *The Possible Humans.* Los Angeles: Torcher, 1982.

Kohlberg, L. "A Cognitive Developmental Approach to Moral Education." *Humanist,* 1972, *6,* 13–16.

Lipson, J. "Microcomputers Applied to Education." In J. W. Green and T. E. Thompson (Eds.), *Proceedings of the National Conference on Professional Development and Educational Technology.* Washington, D.C.: Association for Educational Communication and Technology, 1980.

Naisbitt, J. *Megatrends.* New York: Warner, 1982.

Norris, W. C. "Human Capital: The Profitable Investment." Paper presented at the conference of the American Association of State Colleges and Universities, Nashville, Tenn., October 31, 1982.

Perry, W., Jr. *Forms of Intellectual and Ethical Development in the College Years: A Scheme.* New York: Holt, Rinehart and Winston, 1970.

Ricks, T. "Microcomputers Proliferate on College Campuses." April 6, 1983, p. 9.

Ross, D. B. "Counseling in the Year 2000: A Day in the Life of a Counselor." Unpublished paper, International Graduate School, St. Louis, March 1982.

Toffler, A. *The Third Wave.* New York: Bantam, 1980.

Weizenbaum, J. "Computer Cautions." In M. L. Dertouzos and J. Moses (Eds.), *The Computer Age.* Cambridge, Mass.: M.I.T. Press, 1979.

K. Richard Pyle is a counseling psychologist at the University of Texas counseling center and has management responsibilities for the career services center. He is currently the associate director of the counselor training component of Project LEARN.

Index

A

Academic advising, computers for, 10–11

Academic Alert System, for academic advising, 11

Academic departments, and ethical issues, 85

Ad Hoc Committee on Ethical Standards in Psychological Research, 81, 86

Adams, S., 9, 19

Adults, computer programs for, 16, 53, 92

Advisement and Graduation Information System (AGIS), for academic advising, 11

Aitken, C. E., 11, 19

Alexander, R. J., 49

Alma College: career guidance at, 15; program evaluation and research at, 14

American Association of Counseling and Development (AACD), 25, 55

American College Personnel Association (ACPA), 2, 64, 79, 86

American College Testing (ACT) Program, 7, 16, 53, 92

American Council on Education, 5, 19

American Council on Life Insurance, Trend Analysis Program of, 73

American Personnel and Guidance Association, 55, 79, 86

American Psychological Association (APA), 25, 55, 79, 86

Ashby, E., 45–46

Aslanian, C. B., 53, 56

B

Baldridge, V., 64, 74

Benjamin, L., 45n

Blakeley, J., 13, 19

Bode, K. A., 79, 86

Bohn, M., 46

Boston University, placement at, 13

Brigham Young University, academic advising at, 11

Brown, W. F., 11–12

Bruce, B., 13, 19

Bulletin boards: and electronic mail, 71; future of, 95; in telecomputing, 18–19

Byrnes, E., 39, 43

C

California Association of College and University Housing Offices (CAC-UHO), 25

Campbell, R., 7

Canada, computer-assisted guidance in, 48, 49, 52

Career guidance, computers for, 15, 23

Career Information System (CIS): for career guidance, 15; described, 49, 52

Career Placement Registry (CPR), for placement, 13

Carnegie Commission on Higher Education, 45, 56

Carnegie Corporation of New York, 48

Castlewitz, D., 62, 74

Cathode ray tubes (CRTs), 24, 29, 65

Chapman, W., 57

Chiasausky, L., 74

Chickering, A. W., 16, 72, 92, 99

Clark, E., 9, 19

Coburn, D. W., 97, 99

Colby, K. M., 8, 19

College Level Examination Program, 10

Compuserve, 71

Computer-assisted guidance: analysis of, 45–57; barriers to, 46, 48; descriptions of systems for, 49–52; future for, 53–56; historical development of, 45–48; professional association role in, 55–56; professional role in, 54–55; state of the art in, 48–53.

Computerized Heuristic Occupational Information and Career Exploration System (CHOICES): for career guid-

101